Teach-Practice-Apply:
The TPA Instruction Model, K–8

The Authors

Judy Reinhartz is Associate Professor and Assistant Director for Field Experiences, Center for Professional Teacher Education, University of Texas at Arlington. She is also the coauthor of *Improving Middle School Instruction: A Research-Based Self-Assessment System,* and the editor of *Perspectives on Effective Teaching and the Cooperative Classroom,* published by NEA, and the creator of the NEA In-Service Training Program, *Effective Teaching and the Cooperative Classroom.*

David Van Cleaf is Associate Professor, Center for Professional Teacher Education, University of Texas at Arlington. A former elementary school teacher, he is a frequent contributor to professional journals.

The Advisory Panel

Beth Carlon, first grade teacher, Gertrude Johns Elementary School, Arlington, Texas

J. Wesley Crum, Emeritus Professor of Education, Central Washington University, Ellensburg

Marlene M. Fong, Counselor, John F. Kennedy High School, Sacramento, California

Terry Gillespie, science teacher, Rich Central High School, Park Forest, Illinois

Marjorie F. Grant, Reading Specialist, RHAM Junior High School, Hebron, Connecticut

Harry M. Peterson, Jr., teacher, Gifted Education, Eisenhower Middle School, Topeka, Kansas

Edna Henry Rivers, Counselor, W. P. Davidson High School, Mobile, Alabama

Peter Roop, third and fourth grade teacher, McKinley Elementary School, Appleton, Wisconsin

Elizabeth M. Thompson, Learning Resources Media Specialist, University of the District of Columbia, Washington

Teach-Practice-Apply:
The TPA Instruction Model, K–8

by Judy Reinhartz
David Van Cleaf

 nea PROFESSIONAL LIBRARY

National Education Association
Washington, D.C.

NOTE

The opinions expressed in this publication should not be construed as representing the policy or position of the National Education Association. Materials published as part of the Developments in Classroom Instruction series are intended to be discussion documents for teachers who are concerned with specialized interests of the profession.

Library of Congress Cataloging-in-Publication Data

Reinhartz, Judy.
  Teach-practice-apply.

  (Developments in classroom instruction)
  Bibliography p.
  1. Instructional systems—Planning   2. Lesson planning.
3. Motivation in education.   4. Concept learning.
5. Activity programs in education.
I. Van Cleaf, David W.   II. Title.   III. Series
LB1028.35.R45 1986   371.3   86-12799
ISBN 0-8106-1830-3

Contents

Preface

Goodlad posed an interesting question when he asked, "Why do teachers continue to teach what they teach in the manner in which they teach it?" (26, p. 466).* This question is interesting, particularly at a time when current educational practices are under close scrutiny from so many levels of our society. Among the many concerns is one regarding the teaching style present in many classrooms, which is characterized by the extensive use of teacher talk and student seat work. Compounding this limited repertoire of teaching strategies is the concern that too many teachers rely on a single curriculum resource, the textbook.

We believe that most teachers are knowledgeable about their content and the planning process. And, while they want to expand their instructional repertoire, they need assistance in developing the ability to deliver instruction using a variety of teaching strategies. This text is designed to help teachers acquire and master alternative teaching strategies to improve their instructional effectiveness.

In order to provide an appropriate mindset for change, we present alternative delivery systems (strategies) using the teach-practice-apply (TPA) paradigm. This paradigm acts as the technical framework for ensuring that the strategies presented enhance the teacher's instructional effectiveness. After discussing the characteristics of effective instruction, we describe the TPA format within the context of effective instruction. Then we explain several teaching strategies, present the steps inherent in the use of each, ask teachers to practice by including followup activities in the "Applying Your Knowledge" section, and list assessment criteria for self-evaluation. While each teaching strategy differs, the TPA format provides a common thread that enables the reader to conceptualize and acquire each strategy. Examples illustrating how

---

*Numbers in parentheses appearing in the text refer to the Bibliography beginning on page 109.

each strategy can be implemented in various elementary subject areas are also provided.

We believe that teachers can become more flexible. Rather than relying on a single teaching strategy, they can be better prepared to respond to the diverse needs of students in their classroom by expanding their repertoire of delivery systems. Because the change process is difficult and lengthy, however, any attempts in this direction must be organized in a way that assists teachers. We believe that this text provides the organizational format to do this—to help teachers learn alternative strategies and to monitor their own growth.

Suggesting ways to change or expand an existing teaching repertoire is a complex task requiring a set of common goals and expectations based on information gleaned from research, effective practices, and the literature. Pre-service and in-service teachers alike should be grounded in what is known about effective teaching, including both theory and practice. Therefore, before describing the alternative teaching delivery systems, we present a review of current assumptions regarding effective teaching. We feel that the TPA format, combined with suggestions for implementing new delivery systems, will enable educators not only to make the long-term improvements mandated by education critics, but also to make their instruction more effective and rewarding.

CHAPTER 1
A View of Effective Teaching

THE STATE OF THE ART

The teaching act is extremely complex, yet critics often want to simplify it. In their attempts to understand and improve it, experts and lay people alike have advocated a myriad of models, proposals, and studies describing effective teaching. Despite all the information available, there are those who say that "no one really knows what makes teachers good." For the critics, the research data on effective instruction is described as "a cup half empty rather than half full" (6). For the optimists, the research accumulated over the past 20 years has identified patterns of classroom behaviors associated with successful teaching (55).

The skillful use of the research on effective instruction is an important first step beyond merely knowing about it. Fortunately, according to studies there are strong links between specific classroom behaviors and desirable student outcomes. While many critics are content to evaluate teachers, Medley (44) believes that effectiveness is assessed in terms of student behavior or, more precisely, in terms of changing their behavior. What, then, do effective teachers do that differs from ineffective ones? How do effective teachers enhance student learning?

Effective teachers have been described as having a finite number of managerial, instructional, and organizational characteristics differentiating them from less effective colleagues. These characteristics are based on behavioral, situational, and trait theories of teaching (53). In other words, theoretical explanations of effective instruction are emerging and are useful for concerned teachers. Research studies on effective instruction should therefore guide teachers as they orchestrate their instructional activities and interact with students in the classroom (52). The findings of these studies can help teachers build their "capacity to reach more students and to create a rich and more diverse environment for them" (33).

Kamii (35) cautioned that too often "teachers today . . . base their [instructional] practice on their common sense and intuition about what feels right rather than scientific knowledge. . . ."

Effective teaching behaviors, however, are derived from comprehensive reviews of research (39, 56, 68). By applying the information uncovered from over 200 studies on effective instruction, teachers can identify, develop, and practice behaviors that will enhance their professional performance.

Several major research studies have examined the topic of effective instruction and synthesized characteristics of effective teachers and effective instructional procedures. The findings of four representative studies follow. As teachers review the findings, they might consider their own strengths and weaknesses.

Manatt (40) has listed 14 ascriptive teacher skill areas that correlate with effective teaching:

1. Possessing superior knowledge of subject matter
2. Having high expectations of students
3. Using praise more than criticism
4. Spending less time on classroom management
5. Teaching to the class as a whole or to large groups
6. Using less seat work, but closely monitoring what is given
7. Selecting and directing activities, not students
8. Modeling what is to be taught
9. Using easy questions with a high success rate
10. Teaching until mastery of unit material is achieved
11. Using detailed lesson plans with a variety of activities
12. Spending part of each period preparing learners for learning
13. Providing ample opportunity to learn criterion material
14. Using responses that encourage students to elaborate upon answers.

Similarly, Walberg, Schiller, and Haertel (68) cited a summary of selected research that analyzed 70 different teaching variables. These authors listed the number of studies conducted for each variable and the percentage of studies that showed a positive effect on learning. Ninety percent or more of the studies indicated that the following teaching behaviors had an impact on learning:

1. Time on learning
2. Curriculum innovation
3. Personalized systems of instruction
4. Mastery learning
5. Revision of instruction based on achievement
6. Direct instruction (on achievement)
7. Lecture versus discussion (on achievement)

8. Student-centered versus instructor-centered discussion (on attitude)
9. Student-led versus instructor-led discussion (on achievement and attitude)
10. Factual questions versus conceptual questions (on achievement)
11. Specific teaching traits such as clarity, flexibility, enthusiasm, and structuring (on achievement)
12. Psychological incentives—teacher's cues to students, teacher's engagement of class in lesson, each student engaged in lesson
13. Open education versus traditional education (on creativity, attitude toward school, curiosity, independence, and cooperation)
14. Motivation.

Research conducted by Stallings (63) indicated that effective teachers allocated about half their class time to interaction with students—they explained material, discussed and reviewed assigned work, and engaged students in question-and-answer sessions. They also planned to have students spend approximately one third of the class time working on academic activities such as writing and reading. They spent the remainder of the class time on management tasks such as discipline, transitions, and announcements. Further, Stallings reported that effective teachers planned activities in advance, routinely introduced and summarized material, used a variety of instructional activities, evaluated student learning, and provided feedback to students. Finally, effective teachers conveyed appropriate behavioral expectations and consistently enforced the rules.

From studies they reviewed, Rosenshine and Furst (56) identified nine behaviors associated with effective teaching. Although many of these characteristics are similar to items cited earlier, they refer specifically to teacher behaviors.

1. Clarity of instruction
2. Explanation during instruction
3. Enthusiasm during instruction
4. Task orientation
5. Learning opportunities other than listening
6. Multiple levels of discourse
7. Use of student ideas
8. Use of noncritical remarks
9. Use of interesting questions.

THE TECHNICAL CORE

Research findings about effective teaching are beneficial, however, only if teachers can transfer them into the classroom. All studies cited seem to contain an agreed-upon common map or, more precisely, a technical core of teacher skills that should guide professional activities in the classroom. According to Gage and Berliner (23), numerous principles "have been found to be associated with higher student achievement and more desirable student attitudes and conduct." This technical core, uncovered and synthesized from numerous research findings, provides a concrete image of what a successful teacher does in the classroom. Within the technical core or common map of "instructional functions" are seven categories. A brief discussion of each category and a list of descriptors follow.

Variability

Teachers with this skill view teaching in pluralistic terms or, more accurately, they demonstrate flexibility and adaptability in their use of instructional techniques. A common misconception held by many educators and often supported in professional journals is a "one-strategy-that-can't-miss" philosophy. Upon careful analysis, one strategy does not fit all—students or teachers. What works well with one group one day may not work with the same group the next week. Consequently, teachers need a "pattern of teaching techniques," including role-playing activities, concept attainment, teacher demonstration, and the like. Indisputably, "procedures always affect outcomes" (30).

The continuum represented in Figure 1 graphically demonstrates what Joyce and Weil (34) call a "cafeteria of alternatives" for teachers. The range of strategies is not exhaustive, but it serves to illustrate the broad base of alternatives from which teachers can select. Oftentimes, teachers strive for the "perfect" strategy but soon find that no one strategy can satisfy all types of learning. A sad corollary is that without appropriate help, some teachers stop striving to improve and end up relying on a single strategy. Professional growth requires that teachers become multifaceted learners; an awareness of a continuum of teaching strategies is a place to begin.

Small group activities such as panel discussions, learning centers, and games give students an opportunity to expend energy, engage in decision making, overcome shyness, and interact. Creative dramatics and simulations encourage them to express their

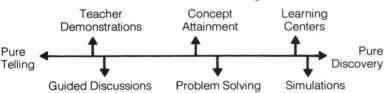

Figure 1
Continuum of Teacher Strategies

feelings, likes, and dislikes in an acceptable manner, often behind the mask of a character. With assistance in how to take notes, the teacher demonstration strategy, using advance organizers, can become a more effective technique to use with students. Other strategies such as concept attainment, inductive discussions, and problem solving engage students while enhancing conceptual understanding.

A word of caution is appropriate at this point. Adding new teaching strategies to one's current repertoire is an exciting, yet risk-taking, adventure. The risks emerge because teachers and students are attempting something new—to adapt existing behaviors to the new strategy. Teachers must trust themselves and their students to be able to adapt after an adequate introduction and after the strategy has been used several times. Also, as teachers and students participate in student-centered activities the noise level in the classroom is likely to increase because of more active student involvement. Again, there is an element of risk, but trust will make perseverance possible.

Studies of the use of a disproportionate number of drill activities indicate that "more" is not necessarily better for producing learning gains (57). By varying the combination of memory and drill work with interpretation and synthesis, learning gains occur.

Furthermore, it has been shown that teacher movement and interaction with students during guided practice sessions—in reading, for example—result in higher gain scores. There seems to be no effective substitute for teachers' active involvement with students. Presence alone is not enough; teachers must act as catalysts if learning is to occur (43). In fact, negative indicators suggest that when teachers grade papers during class time, students develop disinterest and lack the motivation to study the topic (63).

An expanded repertoire of teaching techniques enables teachers to become more flexible in their delivery of instruction as they accommodate the various learning styles. As the old saying points out, "the best laid plans" have a way of yielding to interruptions—

picture taking, loudspeaker announcements, and money-making projects. The same is true for interruptions initiated when students misunderstand the focus of the lesson. Contingency plans are therefore necessary and they do not come without some preparation. Teachers need to have several options ready to ensure interesting and worthwhile classes.

The teacher who is flexible and varies instruction—

a. Changes the pace of instruction.
b. Considers students' needs and incorporates their interests in lesson planning.
c. Uses community resources in presenting subject matter.
d. Provides opportunities for projects as a way to demonstrate knowledge.
e. Develops a repertoire of teaching skills and activities.
f. Provides for adaptable classroom arrangements.

Enthusiasm and Interest During Instruction

Of the teaching behaviors, showing enthusiasm and maintaining interest during instruction may be the most important. This assumption is supported by research studies examined by Ryans (60), Rosenshine and Furst (56), Medley (43), and Rosenshine (54). According to other studies on teacher effectiveness, enthusiasm seems to be responsible for increasing recall, producing comprehensive learning gains, improving attitudes, and increasing divergent thinking (62, 11). Walberg, Schiller, and Haertel (68) found that enthusiasm positively affects learning; there is, in fact, a 100 percent correlation between teacher enthusiasm and student learning.

The enthusiastic teacher—

a. Smiles a great deal and makes learning fun.
b. Is alert and full of energy, excited about what is being taught, exciting to listen to and watch.
c. Is motivated, motivates others, and shows interest in the subject.
d. Maintains eye contact.
e. Modulates voice level by volume and rate.
f. Is involved.

Direct Instruction

Teachers who possess this skill are clear and use a variety of explanations during presentations. The essential quality of effective teachers is a concern for long-term goals. Each day becomes the means for bringing students closer to these goals. Concerned teachers teach with one eye on the future, never losing sight of the goal of helping students become the best they can possibly become. In the overall scheme, then, day-to-day events must be executed with precision so that learning can take place. Students whose teachers lack clarity of instruction do not clearly understand what is expected and do not know where they are going in terms of course content. Deviance and confusion are likely to increase in classrooms in which teachers (and students) are uncertain about expected outcomes (37). It is each teacher's responsibility to make sure that students understand the course objectives as they relate to the sequence of events and the content to be learned, and to provide the direction for moving toward a goal or goals.

Support for this teaching skill can be found in research on encoding and decoding information. Teachers cannot assume that students understand what they are saying because it may seem obvious. When they instruct too rapidly, something happens—students become confused. They need to be prepared to say, "Wait a moment, I have lost them." By reading the cues within each situation, teachers are in a better position to guide students toward understanding the focus of the lesson (20).

Direct instruction is a necessary skill if students are to learn. The teacher who uses direct instruction—

a. Reviews procedures, information, and directions before moving to new material.

b. Gives simple, concise directions and may list them on the chalkboard.

c. Rephrases questions, clarifies statements, and encourages students to ask questions.

d. Uses many examples to explain a point in a less abstract and confusing way.

e. Demonstrates (models) what will be done (25).

f. Paces lessons to coincide with varying learning rates (36).

g. Establishes smooth transitions from subject to subject and situation to situation (2).

h. Expects students to learn and communicates this expectation.

i. Plans, including short- and long-term goals; identifies behavioral performance objectives (68); and writes a description of the methods, content, and evaluation systems.

j. Has organizational skills and attends to detail. Medley (43) found that effective teaching is more evident in a structured,

15

well-organized environment. "Good organization . . . is good instruction" (8).

k. Explains how the work is to be done.
l. Adjusts instructional level to match student attention spans.
m. Structures lessons using teach and practice procedures.
n. Uses visuals, chalkboard, and several examples to provide a step-by-step approach when explaining information.

Task Orientation

Whether the term is task orientation, time on task, or academic learning time (10), we operationally define it as time during which students are actively and productively engaged in learning enterprises that can be traced to well-defined instructional objectives. During this time disruptions are greatly reduced and students are not idle and bored—for example, waiting for papers to be graded or waiting for further instructions from the teacher. It should be noted that in an average school year of 170 days, with 120 hours of mathematics (based on one 45-minute period each day), students are on task for a total of only about 37 hours (10).

This variable has significant implications for teachers who want to become more effective in the classroom. Certainly if students are encouraged to devote their full attention to academic tasks, they should learn. Some educators suggest that more academic learning tasks would result in positive changes in achievement scores (10, 68).

Time on task may also include seat work with the teacher regularly communicating with each student and monitoring individual progress. Within a businesslike, structured environment, there are choices, variety, and flexibility. There is, however, no question that the teacher is the efficient manager of the instructional program, the materials, and the students. This does not mean shedding one's sense of humor at the classroom door. Laughing and joking are still pleasurable activities, in the right amounts and never at student expense. It is also important that teachers remember what being a student was like.

The teacher who places an emphasis on task orientation—

a. Plans activities that allow students to practice newly learned skills.
b. Monitors activities closely to ensure that students are completing the assignment.
c. Has students demonstrate skills to the class.

16

d. Regularly reviews assignments with students and incorporates activities in the evaluation system.

e. Conducts the classroom so that less time is spent on housekeeping chores such as taking attendance and distributing books and more time is spent on developing learning skills.

Use of Interesting Questions

This teacher skill may be somewhat misleading. For this discussion, it relates to asking a broad range of questions that lessen the threat of failure and invite all students to participate. Calling on a student before asking a question gets all students involved, not only those who know the answer (22). Embedded in the teacher's questions are cues that enable students to know the cognitive task to be performed. Kounin (37) stresses "withitness" during instruction. Teachers who teach in this way are in touch with what is transpiring in the classroom. Sanders (60a) also makes helpful suggestions for classroom questions.

Current research indicates that teachers ask more recall/ information questions than any other type—60 percent (24). They ask probing questions only 20 percent of the time. Open-ended, often without a right or wrong answer, probing questions invite students to explore information and supply the appropriate concepts and principles. Such questions are important because they improve student responses and help them demonstrate their understanding (69). As the instructional process shifts away from the teacher-dominated classroom to one designed by the teacher with student involvement, questioning strategies can become useful teaching techniques.

The teacher who improves questioning skills—

a. Prepares a list of questions for each lesson.

b. Examines the list of questions to ensure multiple levels of thinking (that is, application, analysis, and evaluation.

c. Asks students to summarize and draw their own conclusions.

d. Asks "What would happen if . . . ?"

e. Asks students to describe situations and examples.

f. Has students develop their own lists of questions about the topic.

g. Uses wait time (described in the following section).

Use of Student Ideas

Using student ideas (4) is a positive statement to students that their opinions are respected and the teacher is willing to incorporate them into the instructional sequences. Teachers who listen to their students model traits of patience and understanding. They communicate that students are important and have worth and dignity.

Patience is as important for kindergarten teachers as it is for sixth grade teachers. Students may not understand a concept the first time it is presented, for example. Such patience and understanding are different from being a student's "pal," however. The teacher is in charge and never abdicates his/her position; this would result in an agonizing year for both teacher and students. The teacher's job is not to win a popularity contest, but to help students bridge the developmental isthmus from childhood to adulthood. In some cases, the teacher may be the only responsible adult model in the student's life.

Many teachers firmly believe in the use of student ideas but have difficulty implementing this skill. Since there is always time pressure to cover a specific amount of content, teachers can compensate by using wait time, a three- to five-second pause between questions and responses during a lesson (58). The effects on both teacher and student behavior are phenomenal.

The most important of these effects are as follows:

- Teachers have more time to process comments and formulate higher-order questions.
- Students have time to think about the topic and how they feel about it.
- The level of student confidence increases.

Finally, planning a time for discussions is a must, perhaps not every day, but certainly sometime during the course of a week.

The teacher who uses student ideas—

a. Regularly solicits suggestions or examples from students during class discussions.
b. Has students bring examples from home to supplement class material and asks them to comment on each example.
c. Has groups of students plan activities for each unit of study.
d. Has students anonymously comment on or evaluate each unit.
e. Uses a suggestion box.

Use of Noncritical Remarks

This teacher skill determines the emotional climate of a classroom and thus influences learning (61). When teachers harshly rebuke students for disruptive behavior, a negative learning climate results. Despite a lack of data for the notion that a positive learning climate increases student learning, there is sufficient data to support the reverse—a negative classroom climate impedes learning (61).

Students believe in justice and fairness. Wise teachers therefore avoid having "pets." All learners are different, and although it may be tempting to single out "good" students because they are polite, cooperative, and eager to please, students quickly sense injustices. When teachers handle student responses and questions positively and enforce class rules consistently, students are likely to consider such treatment impartial and fair.

The teacher who avoids using critical remarks—

a. Works to develop a vocabulary of praise words (such as "Good comment," "Interesting idea," "Nice suggestion," "Great job").
b. Tries to identify something positive about each student and cultivates that trait.
c. Remembers that praise motivates and encourages students to learn.
d. Provides rewards (verbal and other types) in class routine.
e. Provides corrective feedback.

SUMMARY

Taken together, the seven categories within the technical core provide prescriptive guidelines for teachers. Many of the guidelines overlap and are complementary. It is our hope that the technical core will help teachers discover the most worthwhile instructional behaviors. "To teach is to be able to excite students with information and ideas and to foster in them a lifelong desire to seek information and to discover ideas on their own" (14).

Professional self-improvement requires a passion for excellence and a desire to be successful with children. "Great teaching demands not only hard effort and dedication, but also a profound belief in the importance of learning" (59, p. 49). In other words, hard work combined with commitment and zeal for teaching translates into greater competency and effectiveness.

CHAPTER 2
A Teach-Practice-Apply Model

To help teachers expand their teaching repertoire, a clear focus and appropriate guidelines are necessary. Our focus is on helping teachers acquire and master additional delivery systems. Appropriate guidelines usually appear as models; several excellent models are currently in use. Among the more notable are Hunter's instructional improvement model, Hunt's flexibility model, Joyce and Showers's coaching model, and Rosenshine's direct instruction model. In addition, expanding on Hunt's notion of flexibility, Joyce and Weil compiled a comprehensive description of alternative teaching methods. While each of these models has exceptional merit, we believe they lack the conceptual simplicity necessary to help teachers effect change. We propose the Teach-Practice-Apply (TPA) model as an alternative that we believe is conceptually clear enough to allow educators to improve their existing teaching capabilities.

Before explaining the TPA model, this chapter presents an overview of three general factors necessary for all levels of instruction. Then it describes the Teach-Practice-Apply model as a strategy for educators attempting to expand their instructional effectiveness. Finally, it describes the TPA model in relation to the seven identified categories of effective instruction.

CONTENT, THEORY, AND STRATEGIES

Successful teaching largely depends on expertise in three areas broadly classified as knowledge of the content area being taught, knowledge of teaching and learning theory, and the ability to select and use appropriate teaching strategies (16, 38, 46). Recent reformers have advocated circumventing the traditional teacher education program by inducting content experts into the profession who lack pedagogical training, but they also lack the essential categories of theory and knowledge of the instructional delivery process. In 1964, for example, 1,000 liberal arts and science graduates were employed by the Chicago school district. By the following spring only 167 remained (31). Because of the multidimensional demands placed on teachers, content knowledge is not enough.

Similarly, knowledge of learning theory is necessary. But if teachers are to reach curriculum goals, they also need a knowledge of content and appropriate instructional delivery systems. All teachers have experienced instructional situations, such as in-service sessions, in which the leader understood the way students learn, but could not relate that knowledge to each curriculum area.

Finally, knowledge of teaching strategies alone also is insufficient to produce learning. While teachers are encouraged to use manipulatives in the instructional process, Elkind (21) noted that too frequently teachers do not understand the content well enough to direct the use of the manipulatives.

Clearly, then, all three general factors—content, learning theory, and strategies—are necessary for effective instruction. While we acknowledge the importance of all three, we are assuming that teachers using this text are content experts and that they have a basic understanding of the theories underlying the teaching/learning process.

TEACH-PRACTICE-APPLY (TPA)

The Teach-Practice-Apply approach developed by Cooper and others (12) seems to offer a clear conceptual basis for effecting instructional improvements. Although these educators advocated teach, practice, and apply as a form of direct instruction in the context of teaching reading skills, the model is applicable to other curriculum areas. The following pages describe the steps of the TPA model and demonstrate its applicability beyond reading.

While the TPA model can best be described by discussing each component separately, the authors must note that there is often overlap between each of the components (12).

The Teach

The teach component is the part of a lesson that presents students with what they need to know. The focus is on the teacher who uses media and materials, explains, and demonstrates while introducing the new topic. The purpose of the teach is to increase the clarity and vividness of small and large group presentations. During this component, the teacher also relates the current information to knowledge and skills from previous lessons and the students' experiential backgrounds. Several terms such as "leading," "directing," "showing," and "telling" are somewhat synonymous with the systematic instruction that occurs. A set of teacher skills (clarity of instruction, enthusiasm, use of questions, interaction with students, and varied instructional strategies) are used to create a set of student behaviors and responses (55).

Most instructional sessions should begin with a teach. That is, the teacher should take time to introduce concepts or skills in such a way that students develop a level of understanding necessary for successfully completing the ensuing assignment. A brief example illustrates how a student teacher failed to provide appropriate instruction before assigning student seat work. The student teacher, responsible for a long-i spelling lesson, began the lesson by stating: "Get out your spelling books and do dot two and dot three. I'll be at my desk if you have any questions." She did not introduce the focus of the assignment, nor did she ensure that students possessed the skill necessary to successfully complete the task. In effect, the assignment, rather than the teacher, taught the students. According to Goodlad (26), this approach to teaching is "so consistently repetitive" in classrooms across America.

The length of the teach portion of the lesson varies. A teacher planning to use the demonstration strategy will have a relatively long teach. Conversely, a teacher introducing a student-centered activity or an inquiry activity will have a relatively brief teach and will allocate more time for practice and apply activities.

The Practice

The second component of the lesson provides opportunities for students to "practice" what has been presented by completing work directly related to the lesson topic. The practice component of TPA shifts the focus of the lesson from the teacher to the students, who are more actively and productively engaged. Thus the teacher is responsible for planning and implementing the learning tasks that allow the students to practice skills presented during the teach component of the lesson, and the teacher is responsible for monitoring the students' practice work. Monitoring student activities ensures that each student is completing the task and understands the skill being practiced (55).

The student teacher cited in the spelling lesson, for example, could have first introduced or taught the long-i skill developed in the "dot two and dot three" exercises. During the teach component of the spelling lesson, she could also have related the skill to previous instruction in order to provide a mindset for learning. Toward the end of the teach she could have had the class respond to one or two items in each of the dot activities. Only after she provided an adequate teach should students have been allowed to proceed with the assigned practice. Because students have a propensity for perceiving and practicing skills incorrectly, teachers should actively monitor their practice, intervene when they are responding incorrectly, and provide reinforcement when they complete the skill correctly. Goodlad found that, in some classrooms, the "feedback-with-guidance associated with helping students to understand and correct their mistakes was almost nonexistent" (26, p. 467).

The Apply

In the apply component of TPA students begin to use the skill either with less teacher supervision or with teacher encouragement to use the skill in broader contexts. As soon as students have demonstrated a reasonable grasp of the skill, the teacher should provide learning activities that encourage them to apply it in related areas—that is, apply what has been presented and practiced in class. In the spelling example, the teacher could ask students to develop a list of additional words producing the long-i sound. Further, students could classify the words by the letter combinations creating the sound. Thus students might produce categories with letter combinations such as "ie" and "igh." The opportunities to learn related information dealing with the long-i sound would mean students are engaged in academically relevant tasks.

Homework assignments, too, may be characterized as an application activity because students are functioning with considerably less teacher supervision. Also, creative assignments requiring higher-order thinking may be classified as application activities as students use the new skill in different ways.

TPA OVERLAP, SPIRAL, RETEACH

As stated earlier, the Teach-Practice-Apply components overlap. Consequently, there is an element of practice in both the teach and apply components. Similarly, a good teach will include aspects of the other components. Figure 1 uses a Venn diagram to illustrate this overlap.

In addition to the overlapping, a spiraling effect also occurs as the Teach-Practice-Apply model is implemented. Bruner (9) advocated a spiral curriculum in which basic concepts are presented with a greater level of complexity and sophistication at each higher grade level. David Ausubel's (3) advance organizer concept is also based on the premise that instruction at any level must be related to

Figure 1
The Overlapping Nature of the Teach-Practice-Apply Model

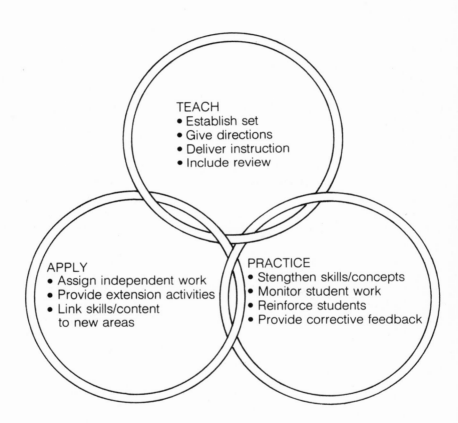

underlying, supporting facts, skills, and concepts. The TPA model supports these contentions as it provides a mechanism for moving from one instructional level to the next (see Figure 2). For example, in an elementary math class the teacher can relate the practical application of a previous lesson focusing on adding decimals to the current lesson of adding prices of four different items from a toy catalog. During the teach portion of the lesson, the teacher can extend learning from the previous level that focused on the placement of the decimal and properties of addition to estimating answers and including the dollar sign in the answer. Students can then be provided practice using the toy catalog. Finally, application activities can be included to strengthen and broaden previous and current understandings as students plan a budget for one month based on their allowances.

In the event the teacher notices that students are experiencing difficulties, a lesson can be designed to reteach the skill or concept before moving to the next level (see Figure 3). The reteach loop can be implemented quickly, and normally results from feedback during the practice and apply phases. Before planning the reteach, the teacher should reassess students' attitude, learning mode, the instructional setting, and the difficulty level of the task. Thus the TPA model can be used to move students comfortably through the curriculum while providing opportunities for reteaching when necessary.

The Teach-Practice-Apply model encourages teachers to be flexible while allowing them to retain control of their classrooms. That is, teachers can use a variety of strategies and still ensure that the essential instructional elements remain. For example, inquiry is an inductive teaching strategy that is considerably different from the traditional deductive lecture strategy. An inquiry lesson should begin with the teach portion in which the teacher introduces the lesson, provides an appropriate mindset or focus, and provides directions for student investigations. Because inquiry is based on problem solving, the teacher should help students understand the problem, identify appropriate questions to answer, and discuss the types of resources available (65). Thus the teacher uses the teach component of the lesson to provide appropriate clarification and direction for student work as well as to convey necessary content. During the practice portion, students, under teacher guidance and monitoring, examine resources and collect data. They also analyze the data in relation to the problem and the research questions under consideration. During this phase, students are practicing problem-solving skills, and in effect, mastering content through the process

Figure 2
Spiral Nature of the Teach-Practice-Apply Model*

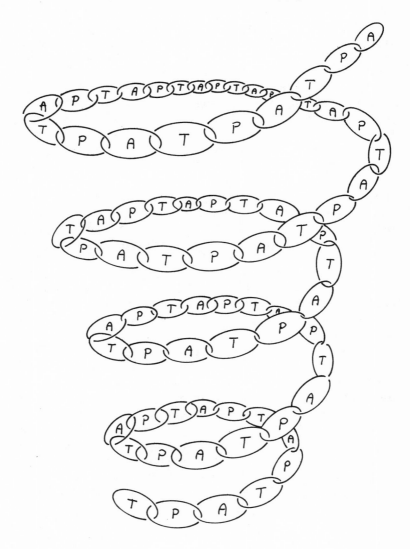

*T = Teach   P = Practice   A = Apply

Figure 3
A Reteach Loop

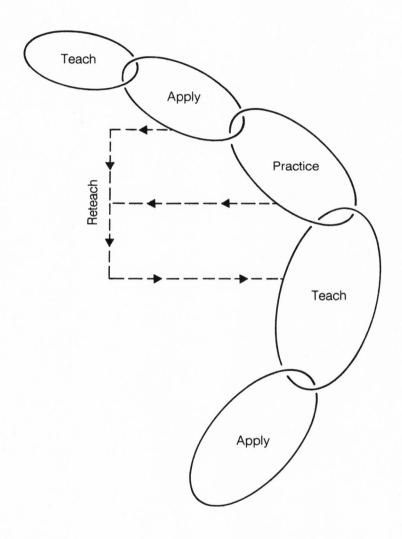

of collecting, analyzing, and evaluating information.

In the TPA model the emphasis is on the application of knowledge—not merely "knowing" it—and application occurs at two levels. First, as students participate in the inquiry activity, they are likely to discover application-type information. That is, they are likely to discover that the problem and data apply to other aspects of their lives. Second, the teacher should reconvene students at the end of the activity in order to debrief them and thereby provide closure. During this component, the teacher should help students apply findings to other areas (generalize) and ensure that they consider the tentative nature and validity of conclusions. In the inquiry example, the apply portion of the TPA model overlaps and occurs during both the practice and the apply components.

The TPA model is a paradigm that retains the best of direct instruction while allowing the teacher the flexibility necessary to use a variety of deductive and inductive instructional techniques (67). Although the TPA components are deliberately planned, the emphasis and time provided for each component vary with the differing teaching methods used and concepts developed. For example, a deductive lesson would have considerably more time allocated to the teach portion, while an inquiry activity would have more time allocated to the practice portion.

TPA AND EFFECTIVE TEACHING

Chapter 1 presented effective teacher findings from several major research studies. It ended with a list and a brief discussion of seven categories of teacher behaviors that were synthesized from the studies cited (see Figure 4). The seven categories of the technical core relate to and support the three general factors presented earlier in this chapter (content, theory, strategies) as well as specific aspects of the TPA model. This portion of the chapter describes the general relationship between the seven categories and the Teach-Practice-Apply components.

Variability

Variability, or more accurately the ability to use a variety of instructional techniques, is the basis of the rationale for the TPA model and for this text. Effective teachers are flexible in that they possess a variety of instructional delivery systems necessary to meet the broadly varying demands of an increasingly diverse student population. We believe that teachers can improve their effectiveness

Figure 4
A Technical Core and TPA

Technical Core (Effective Instruction)	Teach	Practice	Apply	Comments
Variability (Instructional Alternatives)	X	X	X	Includes Planning
Enthusiasm	X	X	X	Assumed
Direct Instruction	X	X		
Task Orientation (Time on Task)	X	X	X	
Interesting Questions	X		X	
Use of Student Ideas	X		X	
Noncritical Remarks	X	X	X	

NOTE: Effective instruction requires planning. Therefore, the effective teacher must plan appropriately to ensure that these elements occur.

by expanding their repertoire of instructional delivery systems and, as a result, begin to view the instructional process in pluralistic terms.

The TPA model is designed to provide the framework for teachers to use as they acquire and strengthen additional strategies. Remembering that most instructional practices are characterized by teacher talk (teach) and student seat work (practice), several avenues exist for immediate improvement. Bennett and others (5) found that very little class time was used for extending skills developed in most classrooms. One immediate technique to improve instruction via the TPA model would be to include an application activity for each lesson. Additional techniques should then include the use of alternative strategies during the teach as well as the apply portion of the lesson. For example, rather than overusing teacher talk, which is often associated with the lecture, the teacher might begin the lesson with an inductive activity, asking questions to draw on students' knowledge from prior lessons and their general backgrounds. A brief presentation summarizing and extending the discussion to a new level of understanding could follow, ending with an explanation of the practice portion of the lesson.

Following the teach, the teacher selects appropriate practice activities. Here, too, the teacher can improve the variability of the lesson by varying the practice activities. These could include traditional seat work or action activities such as gathering data in the library, thus practicing reference and inquiry skills.

The TPA model encourages teachers to view the instructional process in three phases—teach-practice-apply. As they begin to focus on altering and expanding instructional techniques within each of these phases, teachers are encouraged to use a variety of techniques.

Enthusiasm

The TPA model does not directly address the second category of the technical core, enthusiasm. However, we believe that teachers will become more enthusiastic when they see themselves modeling an expanded repertoire of teaching behaviors and also see the resulting positive student responses. Indeed, much like the Hawthorne effect that occurs when individuals become part of an experiment, the enthusiasm resulting from teachers' attempts to begin improving their professional skills will translate into an increased level of enthusiasm for themselves and their students.

Direct Instruction

Direct instruction focuses on the clarity and organization of the teaching act; it relates specifically to the teach phase of the TPA model. The teach phase encourages teachers to focus on presenting information and directions clearly, relating current instruction to prior instruction, using sufficient examples, and communicating expectations. We believe, however, that the teach portion of the TPA model goes well beyond the reliance on the lecture strategy suggested by direct instruction. Teachers can present information using deductive strategies (lecture) as well as inductive strategies (discussion, inquiry) as they plan and deliver instruction during the teach portion of the TPA model. Thus we envision them designing teach portions of their lessons that go well beyond a singular reliance on the lecture; we envision them enhancing their flexibility as they use alternative "teach" strategies.

Task Orientation

Also referred to as time on task, task orientation relates to the extent to which students are involved in instructional activities. During the lecture, teachers are usually the only individuals in volved. Students may occasionally tune in, but most often they are tuned out. For this reason alone, the use of alternative strategies during the teach portion of the lesson makes sense. The practice phase also needs alternative strategies, however. Traditional practice activities center around worksheets and assigned pages in the text. When these activities are overused, students tend to spend less time on such assignments and become bored. Rather than taking time to complete the assignments as accurately as possible and gain better understanding of the skill, they frequently rush through them as quickly as possible. The real task in their minds often becomes one of completion rather than of learning.

For this reason we encourage teachers to consider expanding their repertoire of instructional delivery systems during the practice sessions and thereby increase task orientation. Practice can exist in many forms. Ditto sheets may be used, but experiments, manipulatives, language experience stories, and active research are among the alternatives to consider. The variety will enhance student motivation and result in more on-task behavior.

Use of Interesting Questions

Questioning strategies during the teach phase are useful to encourage students to participate. They allow teachers to evaluate student understanding, maintain student accountability, and encourage students to relate the topic of the lesson to their personal experiences. The TPA model supports research on effective questioning by encouraging teachers to ask questions that relate new information to previous lessons. Further, teachers should ask questions to check for student understanding before assigning practice work.

Teachers can also enhance instructional effectiveness by asking questions during the apply portion of the lesson. Questions such as "How might this skill be applied to . . .?" or "Where else might you see examples of this?" will facilitate application of learning.

Use of Student Ideas

Students need to feel that they are important and that their ideas are valued. Research indicates that effective teachers establish an atmosphere that accepts student ideas.

The TPA model provides opportunities to solicit student input primarily during the teach and apply phases. Through questioning and establishing a general notion that students can raise questions, teachers should deliberately include opportunities for formal student input during these phases. Further, expanding their teaching repertoire beyond teacher talk and student seat work will require teachers to include delivery systems that encourage student input and interaction.

Use of Noncritical Remarks

Accepting student ideas contributes to the classroom climate, as does the use of noncritical remarks. We believe that teachers must develop a warm, nurturing classroom environment. Thus in planning, delivering, and monitoring instruction, they must provide positive, corrective feedback in a way that maintains expectations but does not cause students to fear teacher feedback.

The TPA format does not directly address this issue. Indirectly, however, teachers need to focus on the use of noncritical remarks during the practice phase when monitoring student practice work. Other opportunities to use noncritical remarks occur during question-and-answer periods of teach and apply phases when teachers elicit student responses and input.

SUMMARY

To improve their effectiveness, it is essential that teachers consider recent research findings on behaviors that are positively related to enhancing the learning condition (13). The TPA model directly relates to effective teaching research on the categories of variability, direct instruction, task orientation, the use of interesting questions, and the use of student ideas. The TPA model indirectly supports the categories of enthusiasm and the use of noncritical remarks. As they implement the TPA model, teachers can be assured that they are exhibiting the skills and behaviors identified by research on effective instruction.

Our concern is not limited to the example of teaching spelling, given earlier; it extends to the broader issue of the quality of teaching. In both the traditional and the direct instruction approaches, teachers rely heavily, if not exclusively, on lecture and student seat work. An observer in such a classroom would find students who are relatively passive and whose needs and interests appear to be secondary to the academic focus of the lesson. The Teach-Practice-

Apply model provides teachers with the essential framework to achieve their highest instructional effectiveness and to maximize student achievement. It also provides the framework for encouraging flexibility. It incorporates and *extends* the key elements of direct instruction and other characteristics of effective instruction. It can help ensure that topics are taught, practiced, and applied.

For the authors, the pedagogical sequence of teach, practice, and apply needs to remain foremost in teachers' minds as they make instructional decisions about the teaching act. Good teaching is inherent in the TPA model, and teachers would do well to consider it as they strive to reach their instructional best. The TPA model provides the mindset we feel is necessary as teachers attempt to expand their repertoire of instructional delivery systems.

CHAPTER 3
Concept Attainment

DESCRIPTION

Teachers anxious to add a new teaching strategy to their repertoire might begin with the concept attainment strategy. Joyce and Weil (34) presented this model as an inductive means of helping students learn specific concepts. To use this strategy, the teacher must provide a clue about the concept being developed, following it with a series of related positive examples and negative (non-) examples. Students must analyze each example as it relates to the initial clue. After presenting a minimum of eight sets of positive and negative examples, the teacher asks students to name additional ones and then "guess" the concept. The teacher helps students by guiding them through the examples to reconstruct their thought processes. In other words, students analyze how their thought processes evolved as they listened to each example. This aspect of the activity encourages students to use problem-solving strategies; it also reinforces the characteristics of each example as it relates to the concept.

Joyce (32) demonstrated the concept attainment strategy at a workshop, providing the clue "an item people wear" for the concept "necklace." He began identifying positive and negative examples by selecting workshop participants who were either wearing or not wearing necklaces. After asking eight individuals with necklaces and eight others without them to stand, one at a time, and alternating between positive and negative examples, he asked the remaining participants to give additional examples. Then he asked participants to identify the concept. Finally, he helped participants reconstruct their thought processes as they reviewed each positive and negative example.

We have modified Joyce and Weil's concept attainment model slightly and have added another step (see Figure 1). We suggest that, in this step, teachers briefly discuss the relationship between each of the positive and negative examples and the concept. This provides the teacher with an opportunity to reinforce the attributes of each concept without the pitfalls associated with "preaching." For example, one teacher provided positive and negative examples

Figure 1
Concept Attainment Steps

Step	Description
1. Present clue.	Provides a mindset (Teach)
2. Present positive and negative examples.	Alternates sequence with the best clues first (Teach)
3. Students identify additional examples.	Provides feedback for teacher and involves students (Teach)
4. Students identify concept.	(Teach)
5. Reconstruct the thought processes.	Strengthens problem-solving skills (Practice)
6. Discuss each example as it relates to concept.	Nonpreaching teaching (Practice)
7. Followup activity.	Extends concept (Apply)

of food that is good for the teeth, using a series of magazine illustrations. Most children have heard many times that sugar and other items are bad for their teeth. Using such items as negative examples, the teacher asked why they were in the negative category. Because students responded with "the party line," the teacher did not have to assume the role of preacher. The teacher reinforced the concept attainment strategy at the apply level by providing pairs of students with sheets of paper containing outlines of two teeth. Students were required to make collages within each outline—one of items good for the teeth, the other of those bad for the teeth.

CONCEPT ATTAINMENT AND TPA

The Teach-Practice-Apply format can easily be applied to the concept attainment strategy (see Figure 1). The teacher assumes direct responsibility for the lesson when presenting the clue, the directions for proceeding, and the examples, and when structuring the followup discussion.

Practice occurs as students discuss their thought processes and the attributes of each example. They examine and strengthen their knowledge related to the concept during the discussion.

Apply activities should be structured to follow the concept attainment strategy. In the preceding example, students made tooth collages. Another excellent application activity requires students to collect pictures or words of additional examples. At a more challenging level, students might develop their own activity using the concept attainment strategy for a related concept. In other words, they could develop their own clues and positive/negative examples as a means of applying a concept developed during the initial teach.

ADDITIONAL EXAMPLES

Health

Another activity using the concept attainment strategy relates to the healthy care of the heart (66). The teach portion of the lesson should begin with a clue, "I'm going to show you examples about keeping a part of your body healthy." The teacher should then show eight positive and eight negative examples in an alternating sequence. Figure 2 gives positive and negative examples (pictures of items or actual items can be used).

Figure 2
Positive and Negative Examples of Healthy Heart Care

Positive Examples	Negative Examples
Jump rope	Cigarettes
Banana	Salt container
Stethoscope	Potato chips
Running shoes	Sugar container (bag)
Apple	TV set
Blood pressure cuff	Butter carton
Ball (soccer)	Obese person (picture)
Swimsuit	Soft drink can (nondiet)
Scale	Candy bar
Low-fat milk	Coffee
Vegetable oil	Beer container
Orange juice	Solid shortening or lard

After presenting the examples, the teacher should ask students to identify additional examples, after which they name the concept. The two discussion steps (practice) follow; students first reconstruct their thought processes and then discuss the relationship between each example and the concept, healthy heart care.

36

At least one application activity should follow the concept attainment lesson. Students could develop posters, write TV commercials, design a survey to assess healthy heart habits in the community, or write a public service announcement (PSA).

Capitalizing Proper Nouns

Rather than beginning new skills by referring to a language arts text, teachers can use the concept attainment strategy. A second grade teacher began a series of lessons on capitalization rules for proper nouns by having students dictate a language experience story about all the people they knew. As students generated ideas, the teacher wrote them on the chalkboard. When the story was finished, the teacher began the teach portion of the lesson with the clue: "I'm going to circle letters that are examples of a certain type of word. I will underline letters that are not examples. You must try to determine the special type of word." She began by circling a capital letter of a proper noun in the language experience story. She followed this by underlining the first letter of a word not capitalized. Then she identified additional positive and negative examples. The concept attainment procedure continued as students contributed additional examples from the language experience story. Identification of the concept followed.

The teacher then led students through two discussions to help them practice and strengthen their knowledge. First, they discussed their thought processes. Second, they discussed each of the examples as they related to the concept, capitalizing proper nouns.

An application activity required students to apply the skill in their own stories about an imaginary family that had recently moved into their neighborhood.

Needs and Wants

Social studies instructional units for primary grade students usually include a consideration of the concepts needs and wants. One teacher's concept attainment lesson illustrated basic human needs with positive examples and wants with opposing examples (since the term "negative example" is not appropriate here, the term "nonexample" should be used). Because young children seem to "need" everything, a lesson of this type can help them differentiate essential needs from items that are really wants. The activity also enables children to use the term "need" more accurately.

The teacher began the first lesson with the clue "The following examples and nonexamples should help you think of an idea necessary for all people.'' Examples and nonexamples included pictures of the following:

Examples	Nonexamples
House (shelter)	Kite
Cooked chicken (food)	TV set
Jeans (clothing)	Gold necklace
Shoes (clothing)	Mink coat
Apple (food)	Sailboat
School (education)	Mercedes Benz
Mother hugging infant (love)	Dishwasher
Police officer (security)	Expensive watch
Exercise equipment (health)	Ice cream cone
Water (food)	Soft drink

After illustrating examples and nonexamples in alternating sequence, students were asked to provide additional examples for each category. They were then asked to name the concept. Because students had not considered the terms ''needs'' or ''wants'' prior to this lesson, they replied with synonymous terms and descriptions. After they described the concept, the teacher used the terms ''needs'' and ''wants.''

In the next step students reconstructed their thought processes. They were asked to indicate what they thought when viewing the first example, and how their hypotheses were reinforced or altered with the presentation of ensuing examples and nonexamples.

The teacher began the next step (practice), discussing each example as it related to the concept. She asked why a house was a need, and for examples of shelters that could also satisfy this need. Responses included cars, tents, and apartments. During the course of the discussion the teacher also compared jeans and other necessary clothing with fur coats and other clothing luxuries. This enabled students to examine the subjective differences of seemingly related items. In this way, they had to determine when items normally classified as food, shelter, or clothing might be classified as wants or luxuries.

This lesson occurred during the famine in northern Africa. As an application activity students were required to make a list of needs and wants appropriate for starving Africans.

Fractions

Oftentimes, teachers tell students names for concepts; this is not uncommon when teaching fractions. Instead of giving students the definitions for equivalent fractions, the teacher can use the concept attainment strategy to assist students in remembering the meaning of such fractions. First, the teacher provides the clue: "I am going to write pairs of fractions on the chalkboard. Try to tell me what the positive and negative examples illustrate. Can you tell me the difference?" Next she/he presents the following positive and negative examples:

Positive Examples	*Negative Examples*
9/12, 3/4	7/16, 1/3
2/8, 1/4	1/5, 3/10
7/14, 1/2	2/10, 2/5
2/10, 1/5	1/7, 1/4
1/8, 2/16	3/4, 10/12
1/2, 4/8	1/2, 1/3
1/3, 2/6	3/4, 2/6
1/6, 2/12	8/10, 1/9

Then students should discuss why the positive examples are equivalent fractions. For example, in the fractions 9/12, 3/4, each member of the pair is written differently, but they are equivalent. The fraction 9/12 can be renamed to 3/4, so both have the same value and are called equivalent fractions.

An application activity might ask students to identify equivalent fractions and prove that if the cross-products of the two fractions are the same (equal), these fractions are equivalent.

Example: 3/4 = 6/8   (3 x 8 = 4 x 6)

One form of the fraction is in its lowest terms and the other form is not. By identifying positive and negative examples, students can better understand the reduction or simplification process (2/10 to 1/5) of fractions. After discussing the simplification process of 2/10 to 1/5, students recognize that the two fractions are the same or equivalent.

APPLYING YOUR KNOWLEDGE

An instrument entitled "Applying Your Knowledge" follows the teaching strategies discussed in Chapters 3 through 8. These instruments are designed to help teachers practice and apply the strategies using a step-by-step format. We ask teachers to complete each task as a means of strengthening their understanding of the teaching strategies presented in these chapters. Each chapter has several application tasks; completing them will help teachers achieve a greater level of independence. In the final analysis, individual teachers' effectiveness will be judged in terms of how well they use the strategies in their own classrooms. As with any new skill, the first attempts may feel awkward and uncomfortable. Persistence and practice will help both teachers and students learn to use the strategies effectively.

Applying Your Knowledge

I. Develop a concept attainment lesson for the vowel-vowel phonics rule in which the first vowel is long and the second vowel is silent.

A. Clue

B. Positive Examples   Negative Examples

Positive Examples	Negative Examples
1. eat	1. spread
2. mail	2. friend
3. leaf	3.
4.	4.
5.	5.
6.	6.
7.	7.
8.	8.

C. Statement requiring students to provide additional examples:

D. Statement requiring students to name the concept (rule):

E. Discussion question(s) for reconstructing the thought process:

1.

2.

3.

F. Discussion questions for examining each example:

1.

2.

3.

G. Followup activity (apply):

II. Develop a concept attainment activity for "energy sources."
   A. Clue:

   B. Positive Examples   Negative Examples
      1.   1.
      2.   2.
      3.   3.
      4.   4.
      5.   5.
      6.   6.
      7.   7.
      8.   8.
   C. Statement eliciting additional examples:

   D. Statement eliciting concept name:

   E. Discussion question(s) for reconstructing the thought process:
      1.
      2.
      3.
   F. Discussion questions for examining each example:
      1.
      2.
      3.
   G. Followup activity (apply):

III. Develop an activity requiring *students* to develop a concept attainment activity
   A. Concept(s):

   B. Directions for students:

ANALYSIS GUIDE

Each chapter also includes an "Analysis Guide," designed to serve as a personal evaluation tool. We suggest that when planning and teaching each new strategy, teachers take a little time to personally evaluate their efforts. This will allow them to judge their performance in relation to the steps explained in the chapter. We also suggest inviting other teachers to observe them. Peer input using the checklist can assist in evaluating their effectiveness as teachers practice a specific strategy in their classrooms.

Analysis Guide for Concept Attainment

Did (I) the teacher—	Yes	No	N/A
1. select an appropriate concept?			
2. present a clue?			
3. provide an appropriate clue for students?			
4. provide an appropriate clue for the concept?			
5. present positive and negative examples in alternating sequence?			
6. present at least eight positive and eight negative examples?			
7. present the best examples first?			
8. ask students to identify additional positive examples?			
9. ask students to identify additional negative examples?			
10. ask students to name the concept?			
11. provide the correct concept name (may not be necessary)?			
12. ask students how their thoughts, "guesses" changed with each example?			
13. ask students to state how each example related to the concept?			
14. ask students to indicate situations where an item in one category (positive or negative example) might be reclassified or might not apply?			
15. provide an activity that either strengthened or extended students' knowledge of the concept?			

CHAPTER 4
Teacher Demonstrations

DESCRIPTION

The primary aim of the teacher demonstration strategy, coupled with advance organizers, is to improve the effectiveness of group presentations. The goals and assumptions of this teaching model are to convey large amounts of information in a meaningful way in a relatively short period of time.

The teacher demonstration strategy is a form of direct instruction, which is teacher-centered (49). It provides students with opportunities to observe the teacher modeling skills and then allows them time to practice and apply these skills. With the motto "What is not taught is not learned," the demonstration model appears to offer promise for improving instructional performance and student learning. The increased rhetoric concerning academic learning of recent years has contributed greatly to the perceived effectiveness of direct instruction (15, 47). Using this strategy, the teacher articulates learning goals and makes presentations that illustrate what is to be done during the practice session.

The teacher using the demonstration strategy first presents a mindset and then becomes the explainer. The strategy is predicated upon direct communication between the teacher, who is "... responsible for presenting what is to be learned" (34, p. 76), and the students, who master the ideas and information presented. Second, the teacher models skills to be mastered. The demonstration strategy is a deductive approach in which the teacher presents the concepts and principles directly to students rather than having students discover and rediscover them. Rosenshine reports that "students who receive the instruction directly from the teacher achieve more than those expected to learn new material or skills on their own . . ." (55, p. 336).

The teacher demonstration strategy provides the scaffolding for accommodating unfamiliar information that is then assimilated into the students' existing cognitive structures. The teacher "rehearses" for students the information they are expected to learn and the skills they are expected to master. In addition, before the lesson begins, the teacher presents advance organizers—statements phrased at a higher level of abstraction than the learning task itself. Advance organizers provide the focus for the lesson and help students "see" where they are going. For example, when introducing beginning math concepts, it is essential that teachers treat mathematics as a language with its own symbols, signs, rules, and vocabulary. With this preparation, learning such new material can begin to have meaning.

TEACHER DEMONSTRATIONS AND TPA

In an effort to explain information and demonstrate skills to be learned, the demonstration model, with advance organizers, uses a deductive approach to learning. The sequence of instruction is from the top down. That is, it starts with the teacher presenting a broad view of the concept (a definition) and moves to specific situations, events, and examples. The teacher demonstration strategy can easily be explained using the TPA format (see Figure 1).

Figure 1
Teacher Demonstration Steps

TPA Phases	Instructional Behavior
Teach	a. Present advance organizer(s) (orally or in written form).
	b. Present concept and provide instructions.
	c. Demonstrate skills (use material, ask students questions).
	d. Solve sample problems.
Practice	a. Ask questions.
	b. Assign problems.
	c. Observe how students solve problems, practice skills.
	d. Monitor students' work.
Apply	a. Assign extension activities/problems.
	b. Ask questions.

The first phase of the demonstration model is the teach. This begins by presenting the advance organizers. The teacher may start by telling the students that yesterday the class talked about acid rain and today is going to talk about another pollutant in the environment—sulfur dioxide. The advance organizer for the day might be the following: All living things are interrelated with, and interdependent upon, other living and nonliving things within their environment. The purpose of advance organizers is to integrate previously learned information with new information. They are taught and prepare students to receive and use new information in a systematic fashion.

In addition to presenting advance organizers during the teach, the teacher presents the information or demonstrates the skills to be learned. As part of the demonstration, the teacher provides detailed instructions and thorough explanations as students actively observe and listen. The key to motivating students to listen during the demonstration is meaning. This is ultimately achieved when teachers connect what they demonstrate in the teach to the activities students will engage in during practice and apply phases of the lesson.

Phase two, practice, occurs when students have an opportunity to replicate the teacher's demonstration. For some educators, this phase is called guided practice or teacher-led practice. During this phase of the lesson the teacher provides students with corrective feedback to ensure a high success rate. The practice sessions help teachers determine the level of student understanding. If students are making too many errors, it may be necessary to reteach information or skills. Teachers should work with individual students, but for only three seconds or less at any given time. If individuals require too much time, the teacher should infer that the concept/skill was not presented in a meaningful manner and a reteach session is necessary. Teachers will know if the teach was a success when students respond confidently and firmly to questions and perform well on practice activities.

Phase three, apply, attempts to strengthen students' cognitive structures by asking them to apply the advance organizers and information/skill(s) they practiced. The teacher may want to think of the application session as students working independently. This phase of the demonstration strategy mandates that students apply the new information and skills in a different way. Application activities extend what students saw and did; they also help students overlearn the information and skills presented during the demonstration. Students can rework the new material by summarizing major points, using different manipulatives to solve problems, and examining the material from a variety of viewpoints.

ADDITIONAL EXAMPLES

Division

Teaching division skills can be quite a challenge, particularly for teachers who want to provide manipulative experiences for students. Recently, a third grade teacher was observed teaching a lesson on division. The lesson format exemplifies the demonstration strategy using the teach, practice, and apply phases.

The teacher introduced the lesson (the teach) by reminding students about the previous day's lesson and stating the focus of the current lesson—dividing two-digit numbers by one-digit numbers. She wrote on the chalkboard the following advance organizers: Division "undoes" multiplication. Division is a method of repeated subtraction. Division is sharing.

Then she demonstrated how 42 paste sticks (four bundles of 10 and 2 individual sticks) can be divided into three separate groups. She had the students repeat the process using paste sticks while describing what they were doing. Next the teacher demonstrated a second problem and asked students to solve it, too. Then she summarized the process and stated that students were ready to solve several problems on their own (the practice).

During the practice session, the teacher allowed students to solve division problems using the paste sticks and had them write the solutions on the assignment sheet. While students were solving the practice two-digit by one-digit problems, the teacher actively monitored their work. She asked questions, required students to explain why they grouped the sticks in a particular way, redirected those experiencing difficulty, and reinforced those who were successful.

The apply phase of the lesson was interesting. Rather than having students do additional division problems without manipulatives, this teacher had them do similar problems using different manipulatives. Students were asked to use their division skills in a new way. For example, they solved division problems using Cuisenaire rods and money (dimes and pennies). (See also *Mathematics Made Meaningful with Cuisenaire Rods* [37a].) Thus they had to apply and extend their knowledge of the whole number operation of division by using alternative hands-on materials. The teacher was confident that students understood the process of two-digit by one-digit division when they solved each problem correctly, firmly, and automatically using alternate manipulatives.

In this example, students acquired new information and applied new methods to solve division problems. The teach, practice, and apply paradigm requires that students master knowledge and skills before going on to higher levels. The application phase emphasizes the need to overlearn basic skills to the point that they become automatic. Overlearning is particularly important when teaching hierarchically organized material as in mathematics and reading. Research on effective teachers of mathematics in grades 4 through 8 indicates that these teachers spend more time on demonstrating knowledge and skills—up to 23 minutes per day—than their less effective colleagues (25). Unfortunately, elementary teachers rarely use the complete demonstration strategy. Rather, they tend to tell students what to do without using several examples to illustrate the task, and expect students to be able to do it.

Graphing

An activity designed by a fourth grade teacher to teach graphing skills required students to record the weekly scores of a local football team. (Other data sources could of course be used.) After the team had played for three weeks, the teacher told students that they were going to graph the scores in order to follow their team's progress more easily. Before the demonstration, the teacher distributed graph paper and rulers to each student. The teacher began the demonstration by showing several examples of line graphs that had appeared in newspapers and weekly newsmagazines. Then she proceeded to demonstrate the steps in constructing the graph, one step at a time, while students were allowed to construct their own graphs simultaneously. They drew, numbered, and labeled axes, and plotted each team's score for each game. They connected the weekly scores of the home team with a blue line and those of the opponents with a red line.

Then students examined the relationship between team scores. The teacher told them that they were to predict scores for the upcoming game and lightly pencil in their predictions on the graph. The first class day after the game, students compared their predictions with the final outcome and permanently recorded the actual scores. This process continued through the remainder of the football season.

To practice graphing skills, students constructed graphs showing weekly game statistics. For example, they had the choice of recording total yards rushing, total yards passing, total yards penalized, number of players injured.

Students applied their graphing skills when they were required to construct picture or bar graphs illustrating their line graph data. Thus they had to examine alternative types of graphs and illustrate data in a different way.

47

Mapping

Using the demonstration strategy, a mapping activity appropriate for grades 3 through 6 focused on locating objects using grid lines. A third grade teacher began such a lesson by presenting students with a classroom map and stating that they were going to learn a new method of locating objects with a map. Before the teacher presented the concept of grid lines, however, she allowed students to familiarize themselves with the classroom map as it related to the classroom. She asked students to locate the teacher's desk, the door, the sink, the trash cans. Then she demonstrated how to locate objects using the grid lines. Using an overhead projector and a transparency of the map, she directed students' attention to the letters and numbers designating each grid line. The letters and numbers are used, she said, to help locate places on a map. She demonstrated the use of grid lines. As she located these points, she allowed students to locate the positions on their maps.

Practice for this lesson consisted of asking students to provide the coordinates for their desks, the teacher's desk, and five additional objects. Relatively certain that students understood the concept, the teacher assigned the application task of mapping another room in the school using one-inch graph paper, labeling coordinates, and identifying ten objects by coordinates.

Handwriting

Perhaps the most obvious subject for use of the demonstration strategy is handwriting. When introducing a new letter, the teacher must first demonstrate the proper formation. This includes noting the beginning point, the sequential progression of the pencil, and the ending point. After an initial demonstration, students are asked to practice constructing the letter. Finally, they are usually asked to apply the skill by writing words containing the letter.

Reading

The demonstration strategy is a natural way to teach reading comprehension. During the teach, the teacher helps students understand the meaning of several words and concepts by asking questions before and after reading a story. Comprehension questions promote and stimulate interest, and therefore help determine the purpose of what will be read and what was read. Such questions also encourage students to understand the main idea of a story passage, to take note of details that support viewpoints, and to predict outcomes. The teacher then demonstrates how to answer such questions by modeling replies after students have a chance to respond. For example, the teacher asks, ''What are giraffes?'' and points to a picture in the story she has just read.

In addition to developing literal understanding, during the teach the teacher can present a story or a poem to develop inferential and creative understanding. This second category of questions, to achieve critical comprehension, helps students distinguish between fact and opinion in the examples presented. They also examine the story for implied and hidden meanings. During the practice session they are asked to explain in their own words what the story was about and to draw conclusions on the basis of its content.

During the apply session, the teacher asks comprehension questions that require students to understand at the most difficult level—appreciative comprehension (45). These questions ask students to analyze the material in terms of writing style, figurative language usage, mood, feeling, character development, setting, plot, and use of imagery.

Through literal, critical, and appreciative comprehension questioning techniques during the teach, practice, and apply phases of the demonstration, the teacher helps students decode the symbols and recognize the meaning. In turn, students can use these symbols to communicate what they are thinking. According to Dolores Durkin (17, 18), teachers seldom demonstrate the skill of asking and then responding to their own comprehension questions. She observed that during a lesson teachers spend less than 1 percent of their time in comprehension instruction. Such instruction is invaluable to students as they pattern their comprehension skills on what the teacher does during the teach, practice, and apply phases of the demonstration.

SUMMARY

Teaching skills directly, in small steps, accompanied by an appropriate amount of successful practice, helps students learn skills that enhance their ability to solve problems. For effective teachers, the teach is a time to focus on one thought, to present material in small steps, to state the advance organizer(s), and to give varied, yet specific, examples. During the practice session, the teacher asks questions or assigns a variety of problems to keep students on task practicing the skill and to assess their understanding. The last phase, application, is a time to determine that students understand what has been presented and to demonstrate this understanding in a number of different ways.

49

Applying Your Knowledge

I. Topic: Place Value (concept)

A. Advance Organizers

1. The placement of each numeral in a number determines its value.
2. Any number is possible using the ten symbols, 0–9.
3.
4.
5.

B. What information and skills will you include in your demonstration?

1.
2.
3.
4.
5.

C. What materials will you use during the demonstration?

1. Cuisenaire rods, abacus, flannel board, pocket charts

2.
3.
4.

D. What practice activities will you plan?

1. Given a pocket chart and number cards, the student will place the number cards in the proper pocket.
2. Given pairs of numbers, the student will be able to identify the larger number (greater than and less than).
3.
4.

E. What application activities will you plan?

1. Inequalities
2. Reading numbers
3. Examining another numbering system (for example, the Roman numeration system) and comparing it with the Hindu-Arabic system.
4.
5.

II. Topic: Use of the Microscope (skill)

A. Advance Organizers

1.
2.
3.
4.

B. Demonstration of the microscope (its use)

1. Purpose

a.
b.
c.
d.

2. List parts of the microscope

a.
b.
c.
d.

3. Care of the microscope

a.
b.
c.
d.

4. Prepare glass slide

a.
b.
c.

C. What practice activities will you plan?

1. Newspaper
2. Onion cells
3. Epithelium cells
4. Ameobas/paramecia
5.

D. What application activities will you plan?

1. Measuring specimens on slides
2. Slowing down specimens on slides
3. Drawing what is viewed
4.
5.

Analysis Guide
for Teacher Demonstrations

Did (I) the teacher—	Yes	No	N/A
1. identify orally or in writing the advance organizers?	_____	_____	_____
2. discuss the advance organizers with the learners?	_____	_____	_____
3. explain clearly the concepts and principles?	_____	_____	_____
4. demonstrate the skills expected?	_____	_____	_____
5. ask students during the demonstration to summarize the major attributes of the new material?	_____	_____	_____
6. ask discriminating questions to determine the difference between new and old information?	_____	_____	_____
7. during the demonstration (teach) and practice, point out discrepancies and similarities between new and existing knowledge?	_____	_____	_____
8. translate new information into a frame of reference that students find personally rewarding?	_____	_____	_____
9. provide individual and group activities that required students to apply the advance organizers and to overlearn the information and skills presented during the demonstration?	_____	_____	_____

CHAPTER 5
Problem Solving

DESCRIPTION

Among the major goals of education and the socialization process is the development of individuals who can effectively muster the resources and information necessary to solve problems. Those in the physical and social sciences as well as those in business and the military recognize the importance of problem solving as a means of responding to puzzling situations. Further, each employs a variation of the problem-solving process to make rational decisions. Physical scientists use the scientific method, social scientists use inquiry, business people use the decision-making process, and military leaders use the problem-solving process. Despite slight variations, each of these approaches to problem solving is quite similar.

While an intuitive approach to problem solving is often effective in daily situations, everyone can easily recall poor decisions made because of not identifying the correct problem, not checking the appropriate resources for needed information, relying on the wrong facts, or not analyzing the information thoroughly.

Schools have a responsibility to help students develop problem-solving skills to prepare them for their future roles as responsible citizens. As adults, today's students will be required to make decisions about their world. Effective problem-solving skills can help ensure that decisions will be based on rational thought rather than on personal whim. Teachers can employ strategies designed to help students become better problem solvers. These strategies will help students learn to systematically analyze and resolve problematic situations. With frequent use of the strategies, problem solving will become "second nature," a comfortable process—a tool that enables students to make decisions based on valid data.

The strength of problem-solving strategies extends beyond improving students' abilities to pursue solutions to problems in an organized manner. When engaging in problem-solving activities, students must deal with content. During this time, they gain, practice, and strengthen their knowledge of content as it relates to the problem.

Because problem-solving activities involve students actively, a

53

third benefit relates to the strategy's motivational value. Students are actively seeking information, manipulating data, and considering possible solutions or conclusions. The fact that this process differs from traditional teacher-centered instruction can enhance student motivation.

The problem-solving strategy may be described as a four-phase process. It has also been described by a number of other individuals as having different variations (42), each depending on the describer's personal focus.

1. Problem solving occurs when a problem is identified. It must be clarified and hypotheses or anticipated outcomes considered.
2. After clearly identifying the problem, the problem solver must collect the appropriate data. This step requires the problem solver to identify appropriate resources such as knowledgeable people, printed materials, and personal observation.
3. Once collected, data must be analyzed in terms of the problem. Some data will apply, other data may be extraneous.
4. Finally, the problem solver must arrive at a solution or conclusion related specifically to the problem and the data. If the solution includes personal bias, this should be recognized. Problem solvers should also consider conclusions or solutions as tentative, and should be ready to modify them when new data are discovered.

A problem-solving activity that emerged from several third graders' spontaneous curiosity exemplifies the general character of the strategy. During a morning lunch count, one student asked, "Why do we have to pay so much for such bad food?" Many students laughed and voiced agreement by adding other derogatory comments. The teacher responded by asking students what they meant. The initial discussion centered on defining the specific problem— why aren't lunches more appealing? Students were then asked to suggest several reasons that might explain the causes of the distasteful lunches. They suggested the following hypotheses:

1. The cooks weren't very good.
2. The principal didn't know how to run a lunchroom.
3. The school district made the decision and bought the cheapest food available to save money.
4. They selected food that was "good for you."
5. One student said that it didn't matter to him because his mother said that cold lunches were better and cheaper.

Students were assigned to groups, each of which was responsible for determining the merit of one of the hypotheses. Each group also had to develop a set of recommendations for improving school lunches related to its hypothesis, whether true or not.

As the groups met to carry out these tasks, the teacher visited them to help clarify and redirect thoughts. Resources and data collection procedures were selected, and students proceeded to conduct interviews, collect and analyze information, summarize data, and report back to the class. The class then decided, as a group, whether the school lunches were bad.

As a followup, students invited the cooks in to teach a cooking activity, compared the cost of school lunch items with restaurant items and cold lunch costs, and examined the nutritional benefits of selected lunch menus.

This example illustrates the four aspects of the problem-solving model. First, a problem was identified and clarified. This phase included identifying possible hypotheses and assigning one hypothesis to each group of students (teach). Second, students, with teacher assistance, identified appropriate resources (teach) and then collected data from the resources (practice). Third, students analyzed data related to the problem and, more specifically, each hypothesis (practice). Fourth, each group developed a conclusion related to one of the hypotheses (practice). Students then went beyond the limits of the initial problem and hypotheses. To extend the lesson, they participated in a cooking activity, did a cost comparison, and analyzed nutritional merits of selected school lunches (apply).

Students are naturally inquisitive; the use of problem-solving techniques therefore capitalizes on their inner motivation. In addition, problem-solving tasks provide a distinct change from the traditional teacher talk and student seat work.

PROBLEM SOLVING AND TPA

The Teach-Practice-Apply model can be readily adapted to problem-solving teaching strategies. In the preceding example, the teacher used each TPA component. First, the teacher provided direction for students by identifying the problem, generating hypotheses, identifying appropriate resources or data sources, and outlining the problem-solving steps. Because of the teacher's direct involvement "leading" the class, this was the teach portion.

The practice portion occurred as students collected data, analyzed data, developed conclusions, and reported back to the class.

During this phase, the teacher monitored and nurtured students as they actively engaged in conducting the investigation outlined earlier. In the process, they practiced problem-solving skills and strengthened their knowledge of content relative to the topic.

In the apply phase, the teacher attempted to extend student knowledge and understanding of the topic so that they could use them in other situations. Followup activities such as cooking, cost analysis, and nutritional analysis required students to apply their newly acquired problem-solving skills.

Unlike more deductive teaching strategies, this lesson required considerably less direct teaching. The teach portion took about 45 minutes. During this time, the teacher helped students clarify the problem and identify possible hypotheses. The teacher also helped students divide into groups and identify resources. During the practice portion, students spent five social studies classes (45 minutes each) over a two-week period collecting data, interpreting data, and developing conclusions. This enabled them to practice problem-solving skills while acquiring new information. In four additional social studies classes during the apply portion of the activity, students engaged in application/extension activities. In this example the teach portion was brief in relation to the total time spent on the activity, whereas the practice and apply phases received a considerably larger amount of classroom time.

ADDITIONAL EXAMPLES

Mystery Island

A problem-solving mapping activity for third graders and up is an adaptation of Zevin's Mystery Island activity (70). As an introduction to a unit on Japan, the teacher provided small groups of students with a blank outline map of an island not identified as Japan. During the teach portion of the lesson students were instructed to identify appropriate locations for five cities. They briefly considered possible locations, reasons for each location, and whether they needed additional information. The teacher then distributed a similar map containing information about elevation. Students examined initial locations and were encouraged to change the locations. A third map outlined rainfall and temperature, and students again reexamined their locations. A final map included information about vegetation and students once again considered the appropriateness of their placements.

As she added each map, the teacher discussed students' placements and reasons therefor, asking them to indicate how the additional data confirmed or altered prior decisions.

Telling students that the area represented Japan, their next unit of study, the teacher distributed actual maps of Japan containing data on population, topography, climate, and vegetation. Students then compared their maps with these.

The apply activity required students to make a population map of Japan. When they completed the maps, they were asked to identify five relationships between population and geographic characteristics such as climate, topography, natural resources, manufacturing, and vegetation.

An additional application activity required students to compare population centers in Australia, a country studied earlier, with geographic data. They were also asked to determine whether the five relationships identified in the practice portion of the lesson were generalizable to Australia.

Newspaper Analysis

In this activity students "discovered" parts of a newspaper by analyzing a newspaper published on the day of their birth (41). In the process they developed problem-solving skills through the integration of language arts and social studies. Taking students to a public library to examine each section of the newspaper, the teacher provided the following guidelines:

- List two national events.
- List two state events.
- List two local events.
- List two sporting events.
- List two social events.
- List ten items advertised in the newspaper.
- List four jobs and salaries.

Students were also instructed to interview parents for human interest stories. They were to obtain information by structuring interviews with the following statements: "A funny thing happened on the way to the hospital," "Parents' occupations at time of birth," "Place of birth/residence."

Up to this point the teach consisted of introducing the activity, presenting the guidelines, and helping students locate newspapers. Students engaged in the practice portion of the lesson by practicing problem-solving skills. The apply portion occurred after they collected the data. Following a brief discussion of the major parts of a newspaper, students were assigned to groups of five to develop a newspaper for a typical day during the year of their birth.

Math

As mentioned at the beginning of this chapter, there are a variety of problem-solving techniques. Many times the curriculum area and the age of the problem solver determine the technique used. An essential element of problem solving is the availability of procedures to confidently and systematically approach fictional and real-life problems. These procedures include clarifying the problem under investigation, collecting data needed to solve the problem, generating ways to arrive at a solution, and anticipating possible outcomes.

In math, problem-solving techniques can be improved by following a step-by-step procedure. The following checklist can help students as they learn to handle relevant and irrelevant information and rely on an organized procedure:

1. Read the problem carefully.
2. Define the problem in your own words (underline the question).
3. Identify the facts in the problem.
4. Analyze the vocabulary for clues to the computational skills needed to solve the problem (circle key words). For example, ''in all'' and ''altogether'' are word clues.
5. Select and test alternative solution procedures and computational skills.
6. Systematically eliminate procedures that will not work.
7. Estimate reasonable answers.

Another, more popular technique, found in many math classrooms, follows. It is concrete and asks students to translate (decode) the words in the problem into a visual(s). The visuals represent the whole, not just the parts.

1. Read the problem carefully.
2. Dramatize the problem situation.
3. Construct visuals—diagrams, tables, maps, charts.
4. Decode the problem—What do you need to find? What information is given? Move from the words in the problem to action.
5. Identify extraneous information and information that is needed but not included in the problem.
6. Change sentences of words to number sentences.
7. Develop problems of your own, using ''If . . ., then . . .'' thinking—If John is taller than Susan and Eleanor is taller than John, then who is taller, Eleanor or Susan?

Whichever technique is used, it is essential to provide open-ended activities that require students to think—to analyze the data, develop conclusions, and determine if their solution is feasible. Such activities as tangrams, word problems, oral problems, puzzles, and situations require students to make choices and think through the problem under investigation. There is no "best" approach to improving these skills. What is important is to have students engage in problem-solving activities as often as possible and get them to think systematically—to be organized and to keep reasonably flexible when approaching any problem. These activities should not be confined to a specific grade or chapter of a text; they should be an integral part of every schoolday. For example:

Judy bought three basketballs and a net for the hoop for $75.44. The net cost $8.00. What was the price of one of the basketballs if the price was the same for each?

After reading the problem carefully, the student begins to decode it and identifies extraneous information. Next the student—

1. Writes word sentences:
   1 net + 3 basketballs = $75.44
   1 net = $8.00
   1 basketball = n
   3 basketballs = 3 x n
   3 basketballs + net = (3 x n) + $8.00
   Cost of 3 basketballs + net = $75.44.
2. Writes number sentences:
   (3 x n) + $8.00 = $75.44
   3n + $8.00 = $75.44
   3n = $75.44 - $8.00
   3n = $67.44
   n = $22.48.
3. Identifies a reasonable answer for each basketball, which is $22.48.

Science

The approach to problem solving in science is a little different. It starts with a question that asks the problem solver to think in an organized fashion. The step-by-step procedure is largely missing, but the question provides the direction. The student needs to think about which variables can be controlled and what will result from controlling these variables. Science is a matter of asking questions and making decisions, of reasoning, of thinking. The teacher's task is to help analyze why students answer the questions in a particular way. The goal of elementary school science is to encourage students to learn about the earth's environment.

Several problem situations appropriate for elementary students follow. Each situation asks for a different solution. Nevertheless, the process for arriving at a solution is similar. It requires students to clarify the question, to collect needed information once the problem is understood, and to make decisions about the possible solution(s).

1. *Electricity.* How can you determine which end of the battery is the positive pole and which is the negative pole?

   Why do some Christmas tree lights go out when one bulb burns out or is disconnected? (How can you run wires so that all the lights do not go out when one bulb burns out or is removed?)

2. *Measurement.* How can you construct a classroom map without a ruler or meter stick?

3. Using science as the theme, the teacher can present different situations that ask students to think and make choices, as in the following:

   a. *Disaster on Moon (NASA Exercise).* You are a member of the Moon space crew originally scheduled to rendezvous with a mother ship on the lighted surface of Moon. Due to mechanical difficulties, however, your ship was forced to land at a spot some 200 miles from the rendezvous point. During reentry and landing, much of the equipment aboard was damaged, and because survival depends on reaching the mother ship, the most critical items available must be chosen for the 200-mile journey. This sheet of paper lists the 15 items left intact and undamaged after landing. Your task is to rank these items in terms of their importance for your crew in allowing them to reach the rendezvous point. Place the number 1 by the most important and so on through 15, the least important. Be prepared to defend your choices with other members of the Moon space crew.

   _____ box of matches   _____ parachute silk

   _____ food concentrates   _____ portable heating unit

   _____ 50 feet of nylon rope   _____ 2 45-caliber pistols

_____1 case dehydrated milk   _____5 gallons of water

_____2 100 lb. tanks of oxygen   _____signal flares

_____map of earth   _____first aid kit

_____life raft   _____solar-powered FM
                                 receiver-transmitter
_____magnetic compass

b. *Armchair Traveling.* Take an imaginary trip around the world. Use a large (the bigger the better) map of the world and colored marker to chart your route. Then use a marker of a contrasting color to indicate your progress each day. Post the trip itinerary on the wall next to the map. What did you find out about the people? Any legends? Songs? What do they eat? What are the chief occupations? What was the climate, amount of rainfall, temperature, amount of humidity? How many kilometers did you travel each day, totally? Develop a table showing how much money you spent each day. For an accurate accounting when you return, keeping a diary might be helpful.

c. *Let's Pretend.* Let your imagination go by pretending you are something or someone else. How would you look and act? Imagine you are a—

computer
visitor from Mars
autumn leaf falling
weeping willow
a mountain ready to explode (a volcano)
a sheep ready to be sheared.

d. *Nature.* Hang a bit of nature on your wall. Take a piece of wood—a two-by-four or piece of plywood (about 4'' to 8'' long)—and stain it with brown shoe polish. Cover the wood thoroughly, letting it dry 30 minutes. The wood will absorb some of the polish; wipe off any excess. Use white glue to attach natural objects such as seeds, nuts, dried flowers, leaves, and pine cones to make a design. What are the materials on your plaque? Where did they live? How long ago? What did each object need to grow? How old do you think it is?

e. *Developing Color Images.* Read excerpts from *Hailstones and Halibut Bones* to introduce this outdoor activity, or simply ask questions about color. The example uses green. Other colors may be substituted. What are green things you can see? What are the sounds of green? How does green feel? What are the tastes of green? What things smell green? Green is the feeling of. . . .

Each of these situations should conclude with a followup session in which students discuss the problem and its impact on their lives. For example, throughout the study of electricity, they are learning about their everyday world. What lights up their lives? Whether facing a Moon-like disaster, traveling, pretending to be someone or something else, working with nature, or experiencing color, students are asked to think and make decisions. Only when they learn to think beyond these contrived situations and relate them to their own lives, friends, and world is problem solving helpful.

Applying Your Knowledge

I. Develop a lesson that enables students to discover differences between insects and spiders.

   A. Problem:

   B. Data Collection and Resources
      1. Student-collected specimens
      2.
      3.
      4.

   C. Data Analysis (Students will . . .)
      1.
      2.
      3.

   D. Conclusions
      1. Similarities
      2. Differences

II. Develop a lesson in which students discover the history of their neighborhoods.

   A. Problem:

   B. Resources and Data Collection Techniques
      1. Resources
         a. Long-time residents

   C. Data Analysis

   D. Conclusions

III. Brainstorm topics for problem-solving lessons in each of the following subjects:

Social Studies
1. Characteristics of a good leader
2.
3.
4.

Math
1.
2.
3.
4.

Science
1. Design a solar heater
2.
3.
4.

Reading/Language Arts
1.
2.
3.
4.

IV. Develop a math lesson that features one of the problem-solving approaches.

1. Using visuals, diagrams, and drawings
2. Problems with too much or too little information
3.
4.

V. Using a mail order catalog, make up a set of problems for your students.

VI. In the passage that follows, Sherlock Holmes is describing the approach he used to solve a murder. As you read it, list the skills needed to "think backwards."

... In solving a problem of this sort [murder], the grand thing is to be able to reason backward. That is a very useful accomplishment, and a very easy one, but people do not practice it much. In the everyday affairs of life it is more useful to reason forward, and so the other comes to be neglected. There are fifty who can reason synthetically for the one who can reason analytically.

... Most people, if you describe a train of events to them, will tell you what the result would be. They can put those events together in their minds, and argue from them that something will come to pass. There are few people, however, who, if you told them a result, would be able to evolve from their own inner consciousness what the steps were which led up to that result. This power is what I mean when I talk of reasoning backward, or analytically (A. Conan Doyle, "A Study in Scarlet," in *The Complete Sherlock Holmes*, vol. 1 (Garden City, N.Y.: Doubleday, 1930, pp. 83–84).

1. How should "thinking backwards" be taught?
2. Think of a lesson in which you can develop this skill. Would detective stories work?

Analysis Guide for Problem Solving

Did (I) the teacher—	Yes	No	N/A
1. identify a problem or question?	___	___	___
2. discuss the importance of the problem/question?	___	___	___
3. ask questions that focused students' thinking on personal experiences related to the problem?	___	___	___
4. ask students to predict possible findings (results)?	___	___	___
5. encourage students to consider several alternatives?	___	___	___
6. ask (and help) students to identify sources of information.	___	___	___
7. encourage students to consider a variety of sources such as people, printed material, films, personal observations, target groups?	___	___	___
8. provide guidance for collecting data?	___	___	___
9. help students focus their data collection efforts?	___	___	___
10. encourage students to record and organize their data in a systematic way (using visuals)?	___	___	___
11. require students to examine their data in relation to the identified problem (or question)?	___	___	___
12. ask students to use the data to support or refute existing hypotheses or predictions?	___	___	___
13. require students to develop a solution based on data?	___	___	___
14. encourage students to test their conclusions with additional data?	___	___	___
15. challenge student responses with conflicting examples?	___	___	___
16. ask students to describe the steps they went through to solve the problem/question?	___	___	___

Did (I) the teacher—	Yes	No	N/A
17. ask students to describe their thinking process as they engaged in each step?	_____	_____	_____
18. ask students to reflect on their roles as problem solvers?	_____	_____	_____
19. ask students to evaluate the effectiveness of their strategies?	_____	_____	_____
20. provide activities that apply the process to new areas?	_____	_____	_____

CHAPTER 6
Guided Discussions

DESCRIPTION

Another inductive teaching strategy is the class discussion. This is a useful teaching strategy when a teacher wants to help students focus on a new term or concept by drawing on their prior experiences or existing knowledge. For example, a first grade teacher wanted students to learn about honesty. Although students could not define the term, each had encountered honest and less-than-honest individuals. The teacher decided to help students develop a better definition of honesty through a class discussion strategy by drawing on their concrete experiences.

Before outlining the teacher's discussion procedure, a brief overview of the term "concept" may be helpful. A concept is a mental category of thought. In a sense, the brain's classification processes can be compared to the way individuals store clothing and kitchen utensils. Most people have special drawers for underwear, for sweaters, for stockings, for silverware, as well as closets for other clothing and cupboards for dishes. When we purchase a new garment or kitchen item, we usually have an existing drawer for storing it. If, however, we purchase something new for which no drawer of related items exists, we must either develop a new storage place or put the item in the junk drawer.

The brain organizes information in a similar way. When we learn facts or encounter new experiences, we store them with similar facts or experiences. This process helps make learning and thinking more effective because we generally think more efficiently when we think in terms of categories rather than of discrepant facts. If students are asked to learn material for which they have no existing mental category, the knowledge is filed away in the junk drawer and thus is not readily useful. Educators refer to mental categories as concepts, which are generally related to persons, places, things, ideas, and processes.

As Figure 1 illustrates, concepts have five basic elements (34). First, each concept has a name (we label everything). Second, there are positive and negative examples of each concept. Third, each concept has attributes or characteristics that relate directly to all items in the conceptual category. Fourth, each attribute or characteristic usually has a value that represents the acceptable range of the attribute. For example, Jonathan apples have a color attribute. Ripe Jonathan apples are red, yet they have differing degrees of redness. When just turning ripe, the apples have a considerable degree of green. Later, as they become "too ripe," the redness begins to assume a more brownish value. The fifth and final element of a concept is a definition or rule statement. This is a summative statement of the concept.

Figure 1
Five Elements of a Concept

Elements	Teacher Guidance
Name	A declarative statement by teacher, "Today we will discuss .."
Examples (positive and negative)	What are possible examples? What are not examples?
Attributes	What do the examples have in common? What do they illustrate?
Attribute Values	Which of these characteristics are most important? Are there contradictions? Why?
Rule/Definition	Combine the information and develop a rule or definition.

In the example introduced earlier, the teacher guided the discussion of honesty by designing her questions to help students consider the elements of the concept. She began the activity by stating that the class would be discussing honesty (concept name). Then she asked students to identify honest people. As they responded, the teacher wrote the names of honest people on the chalkboard. Then she asked students to think of and name dishonest people. Again, she listed names on the chalkboard, completing the listing of positive and negative examples.

Using the positive and negative examples, the teacher began to help students identify the attributes or characteristics of an honest person. First she asked students to examine the list of honest people and state the characteristics that made them honest. Then she had them consider the negative examples, identifying characteristics that made these people dishonest. Again she listed student responses on the chalkboard. Once she had completed these lists, she asked students to identify the characteristics most representative of the honest people as well as those most representative of the dishonest people.

As noted earlier, the attribute value element is usually appropriate for all concepts. In the honesty activity, the teacher approached this element somewhat cautiously by first asking students if any of the honest people might have done something less than honest. For example, if George Washington's name appeared on the list of honest people, might George Washington have ever lied? Or if the current president's name were listed, might the president have made campaign promises that could not be kept? Similarly, the teacher asked students to determine whether the dishonest people might, at times, do something honest. This helps students consider the ranges of honesty, from someone who is almost always honest, to someone who is honest most of the time, to someone who is dishonest for the better part of each day.

Additional attribute value questions might be structured to encourage students to consider the value range in greater depth. For example, the teacher asked how students should respond if asked by a friend to comment on how they liked what they considered an unattractive item of clothing. Should they be honest, say they do not like it, and risk hurting the person's feelings? Or should they lie and say they like the item? Further, does such a lie make them dishonest? A more pertinent example might be how to respond to a caller asking to speak to the parents when the child is home alone. As attribute value questions tend to be higher-level probing questions, their use helps ensure a balance between low- and high-level questions.

Finally, the teacher asked students to consider the previous discussion and develop a definition of honesty. Student definitions were compared to the original examples and related to the attributes discussed by the class.

GUIDED DISCUSSIONS AND TPA

When planning a class discussion, teachers must keep two points in mind. First, they should develop the discussion questions before the class period and design them to elicit the five elements of the concept under consideration. Second, the TPA format enhances development of the five elements.

In the preceding discussion of honesty, the teach included stating the name and eliciting examples. As students identified examples, however, they began considering the relationship between examples and, in effect, began practicing the content. Practice continued as students were asked to consider attributes of honest and dishonest people. The apply phase emerged as the group discussed attribute values and as students formulated a definition.

As with other teaching strategies, additional practice and apply activities should follow the discussion session. Students could strengthen their knowledge of the attributes of an honest person by designing a schematic diagram of such a person. An application activity might consist of a student-designed prison reform program.

During guided discussions, the teacher asks reflective-type questions, encouraging students to communicate their thoughts, listen actively to different points of view, organize the information in some meaningful way, and react to the comments of their classmates. The teacher moderates the discussion by listening to comments, checking to see if students are contributing relevant information, and observing individual students. Throughout the discussion, students are asked to summarize and paraphrase major ideas and points, thus practicing and rehearsing content. The teacher's role is that of a moderator, encouraging all students to participate; stimulating reflective thinking that requires students to compare and contrast, apply the newly learned information, classify ideas/data, and identify ways to show cause-and-effect relationships. The guided discussion strategy provides a forum for students to exchange ideas and ask questions (see Figure 2). For a free interchange of ideas, the classroom environment should encourage open-mindedness, flexibility, objectivity, and reflective processes— the fundamental properties of a discussion (29).

Figure 2
Teacher/Student Roles During a Discussion

Teacher's Role	Student's Role
Determines concepts	Compares
Motivates students to become involved	Contrasts
Asks stimulating questions	Applies
Uses media	Classifies
Moderates	Shows cause and effect
Encourages students to participate	Interacts

While guided discussion can be an excellent teaching strategy, several cautions are in order. First, a class discussion is not possible if students know nothing about the concept. Student teachers, for example, often develop lesson plans that include discussion activities when they really intend to lecture. In one case, a student teacher, preparing an introductory fifth grade social studies lesson on products from a particular region of the United States, indicated that she would introduce the lesson with a class discussion: "Today we'll discuss products from the Northwest." None of the students had any knowledge of the region, however; in effect, she lectured about the products of the Northwest.

A second caution concerns questioning skills. Most teachers have been inundated with Bloom's taxonomy as a guide for improving questioning strategies. We believe that good questioning skills are necessary, and structuring questions to elicit the elements of a concept as outlined in Figure 1 will enhance the development of these skills.

ADDITIONAL EXAMPLES

Similes

The discussion that follows is appropriate as early as third grade, or whenever the concept "similes" is introduced or reintroduced. The teacher who presented this discussion used the prescribed format with one exception—she did not elicit negative examples.

The teacher began the activity by telling students they would be discussing a new term, "simile." She asked them to provide phrases that compared two things using the words "like" or "as." For example, as smart as a whip and smart like a fox. After students generated examples, the teacher asked them to consider the examples and indicate what they had in common—their attributes. Similes tend to have two similar attributes: the use of "like" or "as," and comparison of two items that are normally not alike.

Then the teacher helped students consider the attribute values of the examples. That is, she asked students to consider the examples and indicate which were most descriptive and which were least descriptive. She also encouraged giving reasons for the rankings.

Finally, the teacher asked the class to generate a definition of the term "simile." She encouraged students to give a general definition that included specific examples.

As a practice activity, students read a passage in their basal texts to find and list at least four similes. As application, students viewed TV commercials or newspaper ads to identify similes in advertising.

Science

The science examples that follow have modified the guided discussion strategy, treating it in a more abbreviated fashion. These examples contain many of the elements of the discussion strategy presented earlier, but they omit the step involving the identification of positive and negative examples. The ultimate objective of the strategy remains the same—getting students to think about their world and themselves. The teacher presents several questions in an attempt to involve students in the learning process. Students think through the answers to the questions to identify the concept under investigation.

In a unit on weather, for example, the concept under study for primary grade students is cloud types and how they help tell if the weather is going to change. After students have observed clouds in the sky for several days, the teacher presents the focusing question: "How can cloud types help us predict the type of weather we are going to have?"

The teacher asks other questions to assist students in responding to the focusing question:

1. What do stratus clouds look like?
2. What do cumulus clouds look like?
3. What do cirrus clouds look like?
4. How is the shape of a cloud indicative of (a way to tell) a weather change?
5. What do stratus, cumulus, and cirrus clouds tell us about the weather?

After responding to these questions—with some responses more accurate than others—students should be ready to state that weather is determined by the types of clouds in the sky. Some clouds usually appear only on sunny days, others on cloudy days, and still others on rainy days.

Health

The lesson topic of diet, which affects the individual's intellectual and physical performance, can be explored using the discussion method. Students learn more about this topic as they respond to the discussion questions. After showing the ten-minute film *Foods for*

Better Living, the teacher can ask: "What steps can be taken to motivate students to eat better foods? What foods are better for your health? What foods are nutritious? Are poor diets common among your classmates? How does a poor diet affect your health? If a student's diet is poor, will it continue throughout life?"

What should result from the discussion? The following generalizations should be voiced and developed:

1. What people eat affects their general health (intellectual and physical development).
2. Poor diet affects a person's intellectual and physical development negatively.
3. Nutritious foods contribute to proper growth and development.

After the discussion, what steps should be developed to motivate students to eat better? Perhaps a plan can be designed that identifies nutritious foods and informs students of the importance of eating such foods. Or a strategy could be developed that persuades companies to identify the "non-nutritious" aspects of their products (for example, salt, sugar, dyes, artifical flavors). The advantages and disadvantages of each plan/strategy should be treated equally.

Using the topic of eating nutritious foods for a healthy life, students have an opportunity to make choices and decisions after analyzing the propositions under investigation. Throughout the discussion process, students cultivate critical thinking skills as group members cooperate and share ideas. In such an environment, the students' judgment and decision-making abilities improve.

Life Science

When studying a unit on cells, it is not uncommon to focus on the topic of microorganisms. The topic can be further narrowed to include microorganisms that transmit respiratory diseases. The study of such microorganisms concentrates on how individuals can minimize the transmission of respiratory diseases. For example, "Can you name some common respiratory diseases? How do microorganisms move through the air? How are the microorganisms transmitted from one human to another? Have microorganisms always caused respiratory diseases? Can we see these organisms with the naked eye? Is the problem more important today? In the past? Why?" In such a question-and-answer session, students become aware of the minuteness of such organisms, how they can be harmful to humans, and the individual's role in spreading respiratory diseases. At the conclusion of this discussion, students might offer the following solutions:

1. Develop a plan for a campaign to persuade students to cover their nose and/or mouth when sneezing or coughing.
2. Require employees to get regular medical checkups.
3. Require inoculations for students entering school and people entering the United States to prevent the spread of respiratory diseases.
4. Plan ways to curb air pollution—car emissions, industrial pollutants, etc.

Applying Your Knowledge

A. Develop a class discussion for the concept "manners."
   1. State name of concept: "Today we will consider _____ .
   2. a. Please provide examples of good manners.
      b. Provide examples of _____ _____ .
   3. a. What do good manners have in common?
      b. What do bad manners have in common?
      c. How do good and bad manners differ?
      d.
   4. a. What manners are the most important?
      b. Do acceptable manners ever depend on the circumstances?
         Provide examples: _____
      c.
      d.
   5. Develop a definition of manners.

B. Develop a discussion for the concept "fractions."
   1. Name:
   2. Examples
      a. Name situations in which you have used fractions:

      b.
   3. Attributes
      a.
      b.
      c.

73

4. Attribute Values
   a. How can fractions be confusing?
   b.
   c.
5. Definition:

C. Develop a discussion for the concept "prejudice."
   1. Name:
   2. Examples
      a.
      b.
      c.
   3. Attributes
      a.
      b.
      c.
   4. Attribute values
      a.
      b.
      c.
   5. Definition:

Analysis Guide for Guided Discussions

Did (I) the teacher—	Yes	No	N/A
1. name the concept given?	———	———	———
2. provide questions to elicit			
a. positive examples?	———	———	———
b. negative examples?	———	———	———
3. ask students to identify characteristics (similarities/differences) of the examples?	———	———	———
4. ask students to consider			
a. the importance of examples?	———	———	———
b. the importance of characteristics?	———	———	———
c. areas of overlap?	———	———	———
5. allow students to construct a definition or rule?	———	———	———
6. motivate and encourage students to become involved?	———	———	———
7. ask focusing questions?	———	———	———
8. present media examples?	———	———	———
9. moderate (vs. dominate)?	———	———	———
10. provide practice activities?	———	———	———
11. provide apply activities?	———	———	———

CHAPTER 7
Simulations

DESCRIPTION

At certain times it may be desirable to help students experience a real-life situation. Even though it may be too expensive or too dangerous for them to engage in the actual experience, a simulation activity can provide an educationally appropriate alternative. Simulations have been used effectively in a number of situations. The airline industry provides flight simulator training for new pilots before placing them in control of an airplane. Many driver education programs use driving simulators as a prerequisite of driving an automobile. NASA uses numerous simulated experiences for astronauts before a space launch. The army uses simulations to teach each task of parachuting. Before they jump from an airplane, parachutists have practiced the process in protected, simulated settings.

Students have participated in mock elections to help them understand political maneuvering and the campaigning process. Other stimulations deal with profits and losses, ecology, diversity of opinions and values, and basic needs. One simulation begins by announcing that six people will be sent to an uninhabited island for a two-year stay to see if they can pass a survival test. In addition to the clothes they are wearing, participants are allowed to take 10 items, but together the total value should not exceed $200. Students are to decide what they will take and why they will take these items.

Classroom simulations are much like games, and many games can be considered simulations. The element that characterizes a game as a simulation is the real-life relationship. That is, in order to be a simulation, an activity must have a real-life parallel. Checkers can be classified as a game, but it is not a simulation because it has no real-life parallel. Conversely, Monopoly is a game that also parallels aspects of life; thus it can be considered a simulation.

A sixth grade teacher used a simulation, a modification of the Nuts Game developed by Julian Edney (19), to develop a conceptual understanding of conserving natural resources. The Nuts Game requires small groups of students to harvest metal nuts from a bowl in order to acquire as many nuts as possible. Each group begins the activity with one bowl containing ten nuts. Individuals are allowed a ten-second "harvest" period, followed by a replenishing period. During the replenishing period, the number of nuts remaining in the bowl *after* the harvest is doubled and participants are allowed to harvest again. This harvest-replenish process continues for a two-minute period. Edney found that a majority of the participants harvested all the nuts during the first harvest period and were unable to continue because no nuts remained in the bowl to be doubled. He then provided each group with a brief planning time to develop a more effective strategy and allowed participants to begin the game again.

This concept was modified slightly for younger elementary students. In groups of five, four students were harvesters and one was the replenisher. Each group was provided with a paper plate containing ten one-inch paper squares. The replenisher was also given a sizable number of additional paper squares for replenishing. The teacher began the activity by stating the instructions once, allowing no questions or clarification. Students were then allowed to harvest. Ten seconds later, when replenishing was to take place, all the groups had overharvested—no paper squares remained on the plates. Thus they could not replenish their stock and were unable to continue.

At this point the teacher allowed students to ask questions and vent frustrations. Then each group developed a strategy. The activity was reenacted with group members acquiring a more sizable number of paper squares.

Following the reenactment, the teacher led another discussion period. First she asked students how and why the activity had improved. Then she asked them to identify additional suggestions. The discussion concluded as the teacher described the real-life parallels related to conserving natural resources—for example, wildlife conservation (homing pigeons, endangered species), overgrazing on rangeland and pastures, and depletion of oil reserves before the development of alternative energy resources. Then the teacher required students to develop a list of 10 natural resources with suggestions for conserving each one. Finally, the teacher provided students with a chart of a food chain, asking them to speculate on the effects on the chain of a member's removal.

Several steps are involved in developing and using simulations. They include the following (29):

1. Identifying a problem, issue, or dilemma
2. Stating objectives
3. Identifying participants and determining role assignments
4. Identifying rules and constraints

5. Collecting resources to use
6. Including levels of conflict (like a soap opera—adding a character, a new event)
7. Followup, teacher and students discuss the experiences (debriefing).

The simulation process can also be described as a problem-solving process in which participants are confronted with a problem and allowed to react. Their reaction to the initial problem provides feedback that may initiate a new problem. Students react to the new problem that also generates (or the teacher provides) additional feedback. This "problem-student action-feedback" process continues until the topic has been adequately considered. The procedure is then discussed so that the teacher can ensure that the maximum benefit has been achieved and the parallels with real-life situations have been established.

SIMULATIONS AND TPA

Simulation activities enhance the instructional process while fitting into the TPA format. Generally, the teach occurs as the teacher presents the simulation activity, identifies the problem, states the objectives, identifies the participants and their roles, and describes the rules. Practice occurs as students engage in the simulation activity. During this participation they are practicing problem-solving skills and developing a conceptual understanding of the real-life parallel. Practice and apply occur during the followup discussion. When the simulation is reviewed, the teacher helps students apply or generalize the activity to aspects of real life. Simulation activities may be followed with additional practice and apply activities. In the preceding example, students listed 10 natural resources that require conservation. They might also write to an organization like the Sierra Club requesting information about endangered natural resources. Or they might interview neighbors and family members to determine how others are conserving resources.

ADDITIONAL EXAMPLES

Economics

Another simulation available to elementary teachers is a computer program, Lemonade Stand. This program is readily available through many computer user groups.

Lemonade Stand allows students to simulate the operation of a small business. Beginning with a certain amount of capital, students must purchase materials (lemon concentrate, sugar, and cups) to make the product. The computer presents a weather forecast and students set the selling price per glass of lemonade. The computer computes and reports the number of sales for the day at the students' selling price. The program also provides additional feedback stating the ideal selling price for the weather conditions. Students then proceed to a new business day, with an opportunity to purchase more materials and establish a new selling price based on a new weather report. Again, the computer responds by computing the number of cups sold at the new price, and provides additional feedback on the "best" price for the conditions. Students continue the process through ten complete sequences. At the end of the program their cumulative results are reported.

The Teach-Practice-Apply sequence is superimposed on this activity in the following manner. The teacher must first introduce (teach) the activity by providing an overview of the tasks and objectives. The teacher should also encourage students to work in groups of two or three for maximum student interaction. Specific program directions also serve as part of the teach.

Practice occurs as students respond to the program. They make decisions, receive feedback, and face new conditions. Through this "problem-student action-feedback" sequence, they practice problem-solving skills while developing an understanding of the relationships among supply, demand, weather conditions, and pricing.

Apply occurs after students have completed the exercise. The teacher must first debrief them to help point out the relationships between the activity and real-life situations. Examples in the business world might include the production levels of popsicles in winter and summer, the price of gasoline during shortages, and the cost of products such as video recorders and computers when first produced and after the market has been saturated.

In addition to a debriefing session, students could apply the concept by developing "on" and "off" season marketing strategies for seasonal goods or services. For example, they could market winter and summer Las Vegas vacations, promotions for sporting equipment, or advertisements and prices for seasonal foods.

Social Studies

"Pioneers" is a commercially prepared simulation of settlers moving to Oregon during the 1840s. It was recently adapted by a Texas teacher who modified the content and context of the original to reflect the settlers' journey from Illinois to Texas. As students began the journey they were provided with statement cards that outlined the setting and the first set of decisions. For example, they were told that they were moving to Texas in wagons and would need to decide what they should take to ensure a safe arrival as well as to establish a new life there. In subsequent class periods students received additional statement cards outlining problem situations and requiring them to react. In effect, fourth graders had to react to and resolve many situations encountered by early settlers— floods, river crossings, dying horses, lack of water and food.

As in the previous example, the teach portion included an orientation to the simulation. The teacher also exercised control over the entire process by the way she structured the statement cards. Students practiced problem-solving skills and developed a better understanding of pioneer life as they responded to the statement cards. Application occurred during the debriefing after the simulation was completed. An additional application activity required students to develop a class photo album of the early Texas community and its settlers. The album included pictures, student drawings, and written descriptions.

Archaeology

A teacher at a recent workshop described an archaeological simulation project he used with his students. The purpose of the project, "Why do we call it the Dark Ages?" was to have the children work as archaeologists. First, the teacher presented 20 covered slide tray boxes of the same size, arranged in five rows of four. (See Figure 1 on pp. 82-83 for the contents of each box).

At the beginning of the lesson all the boxes were covered with a green cloth. On Day One the children had to decide which box to start with and they opened a total of seven boxes. To map their discoveries as each box was opened, students recorded the contents on graph paper. On Day Two, they opened eight boxes and on Day three the remaining ones. The arrangements of the 20 boxes and the clues they contained gave students information about Saxon society. The use of an archaeological approach revealed the pieces of the puzzle. It provided an opportunity for students to learn about the past—the cultural conflict, the literature, the migration, and the people's use of leisure time.

In this simulation, students, like historians and archaeologists, reconstructed what transpired in the Saxon society without using written documentation. In effect, they functioned like detectives as they stripped away the debris, layer by layer (or box by box).

City Planning

Another activity requires students to simulate the site selection process for a new bicycle manufacturing company (adapted from Hoover and Hollingsworth [29] and adaptable for all grade levels). Leaders of the Philly Bicycle Manufacturing Company have organized a committee to identify a suitable location for a new manufacturing plant. Students are assigned to small groups, each of which assumes the role of a site selection committee.

The teacher begins by asking each committee to generate a list of resources needed to produce bicycles. This information is necessary before evaluating potential cities. (A field trip to a manufacturing company before this activity would be helpful.)

After resource lists have been generated, the teacher calls the groups together and briefly combines the lists, writing a class resource list on the chalkboard. Then the committees reconvene and prioritize the items according to their relative importance.

The whole class again meets to share the priorities, at which time the teacher asks students to indicate the kinds of information they need to select an appropriate site. Then, telling students that four cities are competing for the company and have submitted population and location information, the teacher presents only the General Statistics data from Figure 2 (on pp. 84-85). Each committee is asked to consider the information, rank the cities (if possible), and generate a list of additional needed information. Then the teacher presents Transportation data for each city from Figure 2. Again, the committees evaluate the data and reexamine rankings. This process continues as the teacher provides additional categories of information contained in Figure 2 and students examine the data and reconsider the relative rankings of each city.

The final task for each committee is to reexamine all the data and select a city. As part of this procedure, each committee must identify reasons for selecting the city and prepare a news release for the local TV station. Further, each committee must develop a list of additional items it would like the selected city to offer the company (committee members may be encouraged to contact parents and business and government leaders for this requirement).

This activity can easily be extended by asking students to locate a city representative of the one selected. To do this, they will need to examine maps of the United States and individual states, as well as population maps.

Figure 1
Boxes and Their Contents

1	2	3	4
Empty	A part of a map drawn on the bottom and a part of a picture. A discussion focused on the findings.	Black marks. What do these marks mean?	Empty

5	6	7	8
Black marks	Picture of materials and more black marks. Children record and discuss their findings.	Silver bowl. There are arguments about what all this means.	The arrangement of lines is symmetrical and students begin to predict what they will find in the dig.

9	10	11	12
Empty, but contains a black line.	Silver coins and secondary sources begin to date the material to a particular historical period.	A picture of a mask mounted on paper. Students decide it is a hut of a chieftain because no evidence of domestic living.	Empty, but contains a black line.
13	**14**	**15**	**16**
Black marks	Possessions in box and black marks.	More possessions.	Black marks
17	**18**	**19**	**20**
Empty	Black marks	Shape is complete. The site was of a leader's burial chamber.	Empty

Figure 2
Competing City Information
(Data to be presented in sequential stages)

Criteria	City A	City B	City C	City D
General statistics	Population 98,000 (Northeast), industrial section	Population 450,000 (Midwest), state capital, part of a 2.5 million metroplex	Population 3,800, isolated rural town (Northwest)	Population 28,000, suburban area (South)
Transportation available	On major river, major rail lines, near large airport on N-S interstate	Has railroad and interstate routes, international airport	On old E-W highway (not interstate) and railroad, airport service available 30 miles away	On major inter-state and rail-road routes, local municipal airport
Tax base	State income tax, extremely high taxes on individuals and businesses	No state income tax, low rates for individuals and businesses	High state income tax, heavy corporate taxes	Low individual and business tax rates, no state income tax

Labor force	Unionized, low productivity, highly skilled workers, adequate supply	Unskilled or semi-skilled, chiefly unionized, supply large, high unemployment	Heavily unionized with timber background, unskilled to skilled workers, low supply	Unskilled and semi-skilled workers, no unions, adequate work force
Utilities	Expensive electricity, water adequate, low supply of gas	Low rates, abundant supplies of electricity, water	Adequate supplies, high rates	Electricity rates low, adequate supplies of gas and water
School system	Above average scores on standardized tests, meets state standards, older buildings	Quality inconsistent, but generally adequate with average test scores, some new buildings	Quality education with limited facilities	Quality above average, funding for education low, but improving (new state law passed)

SUMMARY

Simulations attempt to represent reality, as students engage in real-life situations. These strategies depict consumer behavior, historical events, present-day society, economic relations, and a variety of other conditions. A form of problem solving, the simulation begins with a complex situation that requires a problem to be resolved as the situation develops. In this learning-by-doing approach, students learn how to solve problems. "The simulation incorporates both role playing and dramatic play in addition to a third element—a game" (29, p. 140).

Applying Your Knowledge

I. Modify the game Monopoly to represent events, places, and problems related to your community.

II. Plan a simulation

A. Area of curriculum: Social Studies
Unit: Geography of a city and its effect on growth

B. Objectives/goals: The students will be able to—
1. work effectively in groups.
2. develop a plan to resolve the problem of competing forces within a city as the city grows.
3. analyze how geography affects the growth of a city.
4. determine how these geographical features enhance or hinder the growth of a city.

C. Concepts
1. Geography of a city can help or hinder its growth.
2. The type, kind, and number of industries affect the growth of a city.
3. The long-term planning of city leaders and citizens affect the way a city grows.

D. Develop a simulation to help students understand that geographical features and other factors work together in determining the growth of a city (this is the problem).
1. Identify participants
a.
b.
c.

2. Determine role assignments

    a.

    b.

    c.

3. Identify rules and constraints

    a.

    b.

    c.

4. Collect resources

    a.

    b.

    c.

5. Develop an outline of simulation

6. Followup discussion

    a.

    b.

    c.

III. You are a seed planted in ideal soil, but you do not get enough rainfall, the winds are gusty, and the weeds crowd out the other plants. In short, life is difficult.

A. Identify the problem

B. State the objectives

    1.

    2.

    3.

C. Determine the role assignments for participants

    1.

    2.

    3.

D. Identify rules

    1.

    2.

    3.

E. Collect resources

F. Develop an outline

G. Followup discussion

Analysis Guide for Simulations

Did (I) the teacher—	Yes	No	N/A
1. present a problem that parallels a real-life situation related to the topic under investigation?	_____	_____	_____
2. state the objectives and prepare an outline of the simulation?	_____	_____	_____
3. identify participants and their roles?	_____	_____	_____
4. describe the rules for conducting the simulation?	_____	_____	_____
5. state the relationships among the diverse elements of the simulation?	_____	_____	_____
6. provide enough time to engage in the activity (time to consider the real-life parallels)?	_____	_____	_____
7. describe step-by-step sequence of the activity?	_____	_____	_____
8. provide the resources for the simulation (money, clothes, etc.)?	_____	_____	_____
9. provide opportunities for application activities to develop realistic suggestions for avoiding similar situations in the future?	_____	_____	_____
10. provide a post-simulation discussion in which there is resolution (within limits) of the problem under study?	_____	_____	_____

CHAPTER 8
Related Teaching Strategies

The teaching strategies and examples discussed in the previous chapters are intended to help teachers develop a basic set of instructional delivery systems. Each strategy is presented within the Teach-Practice-Apply format, and each is accompanied by examples appropriate for elementary classrooms. This chapter presents additional ideas and strategies—learning centers, role playing, independent study, and small group work.

The learning center approach is an excellent alternative to other instructional formats such as large group instruction. It enables students to learn concepts and practice skills with a greater degree of enthusiasm and independence. In role playing, students can become actively involved as they assume another's perspective. Independent study offers teachers a strategy for guiding one or more students as they pursue topics that are often of a personal interest. Finally, small group work provides options for students to work together, learn from one another, and cooperatively solve problems.

LEARNING CENTERS

A learning center or instructional resource center (29) is an area or place in a classroom in which students work individually or cooperatively in small groups to accomplish a task. Each center should (1) include motivating, self-directing, and self-checking activities designed for students at varying learning and maturity levels; (2) provide students with choices or alternatives; and (3) contain a varied and extensive collection of learning resources in the form of media, textbooks, articles, manipulatives, maps, globes, laboratory supplies, and educational technology.

In the planning stages, the teacher decides on the specific skills and content to be introduced, taught, and/or reinforced in the learning center. Next, the instructional objectives need to be identified and the materials collected. The final step is to construct the center, considering such elements as blank wall space, bulletin boards, the inside of closet doors, and space below tables when choosing the location. Poster board centers can be constructed by folding a 14'' x 22'' poster board in half, making the center 14 inches tall with two parts 11 inches wide. Folding ensures that the poster board will stand freely. Each center should be attractive, and should include grammatically correct signs and directions for students.

The following checklist may be helpful as teachers prepare the individual components of the center.

Checklist for Setting Up a Learning Center

_____ A. Are the center activities, experiments, and games based on clearly stated instructional objectives?

_____ B. Have you provided a chart that gives directions clearly and lists procedures to be followed in completing the center activities?

_____ C. Are the activities easy to follow? Do you have step-by-step instructions?

_____ D. Are the activities developed in such a way that they require minimum teacher assistance?

_____ E. Is the center designed to provide adequate working space? Have you included all materials?

_____ F. Are self-evaluation techniques supplied for those activities that require immediate checking?

_____ G. Does the center include multilevel activities, experiments, and games to meet the needs, abilities, and interests of a variety of students?

_____ H. Does the center motivate by providing—

    _____ challenging and creative tasks?

    _____ a large clear title?

    _____ questions?

    _____ colorful and appropriate illustrations?

    _____ directions and activities large enough to be seen easily?

    _____ neat lettering and arrangement with no grammatical errors?

_____ I. How will you evaluate student learning?

    _____ What will be turned in for a grade? for your review?

    _____ How will you know what students have learned?

The center approach adds color and excitement to learning and stimulates interest in the topic under investigation. The final measure of its success is student use of the center during the schoolday.

LEARNING CENTERS AND TPA

The teacher predetermines the topic, the concepts, and the choices for each learning center. During the teach, students become aware of the purpose of each center and receive procedural information (acceptable number of students at each center at a given time, time limit, self-checking) and specific instructions for successfully completing the individual activities. The teach affords students the opportunity to ask questions if they do not understand. Therefore, before students begin their center work they have the essential elements to accomplish each task with a minimum of teacher input and guidance. A directive approach in the beginning ensures that students understand what they are expected to do.

While working at the centers, students have several opportunities, independently or in pairs, to practice and apply the skills taught. The activities should be designed to give them the confidence they need to master the skills presented earlier. The teacher monitors individual work to ensure that each student is on task, to answer questions students may have, and to provide feedback. The interplay between students as they work at the center encourages them to express their ideas and develop a strategy to convince others that their positions are valid and their work is meaningful.

At the end of the practice and apply sessions, the teacher can conduct a debriefing session to discuss what students have learned and how it has affected their thinking. This review session can clarify terms, concepts, or questions.

A center approach was used to introduce "Investigating Your Environment," a topic suitable for grades 3 through 8. Students were asked to think about their surroundings and to use the classroom and the natural environment as the learning laboratory (50).

The key concepts presented during the teach were as follows:

1. All living things are interrelated and interdependent upon other living and nonliving things within the environment.
2. Humans and all their activities are important elements in influencing changes that affect all other living and nonliving things; these changes can enhance, destroy, or leave the natural conditions unaffected through time.
3. Change can be viewed as a continuous process through which living and nonliving matter undergoes predictable phases of birth (origin), maturation, decline, and death.
4. Living things are capable of responding to changes in their environment.

Four centers were constructed to assist students in learning more about their world: an activity center, a resource center, a creative center, and a publishing center. The teacher briefly explained the purpose of these centers, told students what they were expected to do, and answered their questions.

In the *activity center,* students played various games (the "Extinction Game," the "Redwood Controversy") and did crossword puzzles. They thought about new terms and the human role in impacting the environment; they also considered environmental conflicts and made choices.

In the *resource center* the materials included articles ("A River Restored: Oregon's Willamette," "Can We Save Our Salt Marshes"), magazines (*Audubon, Sierra Club Bulletin*), tapes and filmstrips (*Man in Ecosystems, Human Communities, Destroying the Future*), slides of different biomes, comic books, records, and books (*Silent Spring*). These resources offered students many different ways to learn about their environment. They could read about it, listen to sounds from it, and look at its beauty and its destruction.

The *creative center* asked students to describe the type of environment they would like to live in and help build. Here students needed to think about and take a stand on environmental issues by identifying problems and designing a plan of action for improving or even eliminating these problems in their immediate community. This center took students into the community to interview people in order to familiarize them with the issues.

At the *publishing center* students wrote their own articles, poems, and essays on some aspect of an environmental issue. They were also asked to express their ideas in sketches or pictures and to provide captions for photographs. This culminating activity asked them to apply what they learned.

ROLE PLAYING

Role playing is closely associated with simulations. During a role-playing session, students assume another person's identity to better understand the person's feelings, values, and attitudes. While "playing" different characters in a variety of circumstances, students have an opportunity to act out conflict, disagreement, resolution, and cooperation. In addition, role playing can stimulate oral communication, creative thinking skills, and creative movement.

Students who are not directly involved with the role play need to listen and observe closely so that they are prepared to respond to questions: "Do you agree with Bill and the action he took? What, in your opinion, is the best way to resolve his problem? What choices are available to Rhoda for changing the situation?"

A science topic that might be introduced effectively with role playing is the selection of appropriate energy sources—including geothermal, solar, wind, nuclear and synthetic fuel—for the year 2000. During the teach, students can consider these energy possibilities in terms of cost—the time it takes to process the fuel, and the cost to ready it for consumer use—its impact on the environment, and public health and safety.

The teacher can divide the class into smaller groups, each of which studies different energy sources and addresses issues of cost, processing time, environmental impact, and public safety. During the practice, the teacher can provide students with options for presenting their findings to the class.

Students should then be placed in role-playing situations as they serve on a panel to debate the issues of energy for the future. One student can role play an energy company advocate, another a government regulatory agent, still another a citizen against nuclear energy who is concerned about the environment, and another a botanist who is the head of a local conservation group. The botanist has evidence that the operations of the energy company resulted in a recent fishkill in the local pond, and is threatening to bring the energy company to court.

Each person must convince the rest of the class of the validity of his/her position, based on the arguments presented. Class members then decide which energy sources are the most economical and the safest for humans and the environment in the twenty-first century.

INDEPENDENT STUDY

A stimulating alternative to traditional teaching strategies is independent study. On those occasions when students are capable of studying a topic on their own or with a partner, this technique is both challenging and appropriate. For example, three fifth graders who had read an article about solar heaters became fascinated with the topic. The teacher, wishing to nurture and direct the excitement, helped the students design an independent investigation of solar energy and solar heaters.

Using the independent study format illustrated in Figure 1, the teacher had the students identify four questions they wanted answered. Then he helped them identify and list possible resources for each question. Finally, he asked the students to determine a format

Figure 1

Independent Study Format

Questions	Possible Resources	Illustrating Activity
1.	a. b. c.	1.
2.	a. b. c.	2.
3.	a. b. c.	3.
4.	a. b. c.	4.

Adapted from David Van Cleaf, "Guiding Student Inquiry," *Social Studies* (May–June 1984).

for representing (illustrating) the answers to each question. During the science period, while the teacher and remainder of the class participated in a science unit, the three students worked on their solar energy project. They were allowed to go to the library and were encouraged to approach the teacher when he had an available moment during, before, or after class.

This process has also been used by students interested in such topics as the metric system, educating the blind, architecture as an occupation, the life of Mohammed Ali, culinary contributions of ethnic groups, the influence of chemistry in our daily lives, how airplanes fly, how bridges are designed, and the books of Marguerite Henry. Almost any topic in which students express an interest can be adapted to an independent study format.

A good example is an independent study conducted by Kelly. After her third grade class had completed a basal reading excerpt about Helen Keller, Kelly became fascinated with blind people, literally pestering the teacher for additional time to learn about them. Rather than allocate additional class time, the teacher suggested an independent study option. With "Blind People" as her topic, Kelly identified several study questions:

1. How do blind people learn to move about?
2. Why do people become blind?
3. How are blind children taught in school?

Once the questions were identified, teacher and student began to consider information sources. In addition to traditional print sources such as books and encyclopedias, they identified the school district's consultant for handicapped education, an elementary school teacher responsible for teaching blind students, and a blind person living near the school. A visit to a facility for training people losing their vision was an additional resource.

As with the inquiry format, Kelly was required to develop a product representing information on each question. Products included teaching classmates to read braille, a series of posters warning about the causes of blindness, and a brochure describing teaching strategies and equipment used with blind children.

The independent study format coincides with Teach-Practice-Apply. The teach occurs as the teacher helps students determine the questions, resources, and activities illustrating their investigations. Learning occurs throughout the process; therefore, practice is integrated throughout. Apply occurs as students develop ways to illustrate answers to their questions. Possible illustrations include models, graphs, charts, poems, stories, games, and reports.

SMALL GROUP WORK

The concept of grouping generally conjures up two thoughts, ability grouping and small group work. This section focuses on small group work. With the dominant instructional mode teacher talk and student seat work, it is clear that the dominant interaction flow in the classroom is unilateral, from teacher to student. This does little to encourage learning that can best occur through student-to-student interaction. For example, cooperation, sharing, and language skills are enhanced as students work together sharing ideas and testing their ideas on one another. Further, the problem-solving process is enhanced as students work together because each one brings a somewhat unique perspective to the group and can view the problem and possible solutions somewhat differently. Thus group work, if managed well, can result in more thorough, more appropriate, and more creative learning.

Suggestions for Success

Students must learn how to work in groups. If they are merely told to move into groups and perform some general task or discuss a general topic, most groups will fail—and teachers may quickly conclude that the strategy is not effective. Group work can be successful when teachers first teach students how to use it. They can accomplish this by carefully selecting activities appropriate for this strategy. Students need not complete a reading assignment or a worksheet as a small group task. But group members can be asked to brainstorm, identify major points, determine alternate solutions, and prepare visual aids for class presentations.

Initially, groups should be small—with two or three students in each. Larger groups make it easy for some students not to contribute. Also, group activities should be relatively short at the beginning of the year. Brief and specific tasks will help ensure success as students have a relatively direct focus with little time to get off track. As their ability to work well together develops, they will be able to manage longer group assignments.

Early success also requires considerable teacher monitoring. By actively moving from group to group, the teacher communicates two messages: (1) on-task behavior is expected and reinforced, (2) off-task behavior will be noticed and redirected.

Small Group Tasks

Small groups can be effective in many settings. For example, group work can enhance a students' writing skills. Writing is a process of communicating ideas to others. Working in groups with a built-in link between verbal and written communication, students can generate draft copies, read ideas to each other, and edit each other's work.

Inquiry activities are also appropriate for group work. The Mystery Island idea described in Chapter 5 required small groups of students to consider possible locations for the island's major population centers. Because students had very little data, they had to rely on personal knowledge. As they worked together in groups, they were able to generate a greater number of hypotheses and questions.

Many science activities lend themselves to group work. For example, as students conduct experiments, they can ensure that the procedures are followed. Further, they can consider outcomes and explanations for outcomes more spontaneously than if they were working individually.

Texas has recently mandated the inclusion of manipulatives in the mathematics curriculum. Students can use these manipulatives in small group settings. As they manipulate the objects, they can talk about the math operation and how it relates to the skill being taught by the teacher. They may also *discover* related concepts such as reciprocal operations.

Applying Your Knowledge

I. Learning Centers

   A. Unit: Geometry

      Topic: Geometric figures

   B. Goals/objectives

      1. State the characteristics of each shape.

      2. Define the term "polygon" and provide at least four examples.

      3.

      4.

   C. Centers

      1. Geometric shapes

         a. View the filmstrip *Introducing Shapes, Lines, and Angles,* CORP, 1966, color.

         b. Identify the geometric shapes made of poster board and match each shape to those on the walls of the learning center.

         c. Play Geometric Bingo

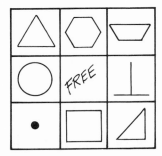

      2. Polygons

         a. Using toothpicks and miniature marshmallows, construct polygons of different shapes.

        b.

        c.

    3. Quadrilaterals

        a.

        b.

        c.

II. Learning Centers

    A. Unit: "Phylum Arthropoda and I Thought They Were Only Bugs"
    Topic: Class Insecta

    B. Goals/objectives

        1.

        2.

        3.

    C. Centers

      1. What are Arthropods?

        a. Using several preserved specimens of arthropods (insects, spiders, lobsters, crabs, millipedes, centipedes) and hand lenses, the students will identify, in writing, the characteristics they observe.

        b. Use the resource material provided to find out more information about the arthropods.

        c.

        d.

      2. Insects

        a.

        b.

        c.

      3. Spiders

        a.

        b.

        c.

III. Role Play

    A. Outline a role-playing activity for the topic "Police as Helpers."

      1. Situation: Investigating an automobile accident

      2. Characters:

      3. Scenario:

4. Followup discussion questions

   a.

   b.

   c.

B. Outline a followup practice and apply activity.

   1.

   2.

   3.

   4.

IV. Independent Study

   A. Outline an independent study related to seat belts as safety devices.

     1. Topic: Seat Belts

     2. Research questions

       a. How many people wear seat belts?

       b.

       c.

     3. List possible resources for the preceding questions.

       a.

       b.

       c.

     4. List possible concrete activities students can develop to illustrate the findings for these research questions.

       a.

       b.

       c.

V. Small Group Work

   A. Identify an activity appropriate for small group work in science.

   B. List the objectives.

   C. Identify the rules for the groups.

   D. Outline the small group task.

   E. Describe the manner in which the small group's findings will be reported.

Analysis Guide for Related Strategies

Did (I) the teacher—	Yes	No	N/A

Learning Centers

1. decide on the specific skills and content to be introduced, taught, and reinforced?
2. establish the objectives and collect the materials?
3. construct centers that are visually appealing, with space for a group of students to work?
4. clearly explain the proper routine, conduct, and general ground rules students need to observe at the centers?
5. communicate what students are expected to do at each center?

Role Playing

1. provide suitable characters for students to portray?
2. provide opportunities for students to role play difficult circumstances that include conflict and disagreement?
3. prepare questions for spectators to keep them involved during the role-playing session?
4. conduct a followup discussion?

Independent Study

1. provide or help students select a topic?
2. provide or help students select research questions?
3. help students identify resources?
4. help students identify possible illustrating activities?
5. establish time for independent work?
6. regularly monitor students' progress?

Did (I) the teacher—	Yes	No	N/A

Small Group Work

1. select an activity appropriate for small group work? _____ _____ _____
2. state guidelines (rules) for small group work? _____ _____ _____
3. provide sufficient time (not too much or too little)? _____ _____ _____
4. monitor small groups as they worked? _____ _____ _____
5. follow up/extend the small group work? _____ _____ _____

CHAPTER 9
Putting It All Together

This final chapter is divided into two parts. The first part describes the effects of the ideas presented in the preceding chapters on students. Specifically it examines how the TPA model and the instructional strategies enhance student achievement, develop critical thinking skills, and improve student attitudes toward school and learning. The second part, a self-help section, provides suggestions for pulling one's own strings—that is, traversing the road to change and professional improvement.

TPA AND ITS IMPACT ON STUDENTS

Effective instruction must be judged in terms of students' achievement as well as of their abilities to use the skills and content learned in the classroom. Student achievement should not, however, be limited to the traditional three R's. Critical thinking, the fourth R, is an essential goal of education. Critical thinking can best be defined as the ability to analyze and solve problems. In a democratic society, adults must not only be able to read, write, and compute, they must also be able to use such skills to assess and resolve personal, professional, and community problems.

Effective instruction also must be judged in relation to students' attitudes toward school and the subject areas. Little is accomplished if a skill or concept is taught in such a way that students dislike the material.

We believe that the ideas described in the previous chapters can contribute to these three conditions for judging instructional success—student achievement, critical thinking, and attitude toward school. The sections that follow discuss each condition briefly.

Student Achievement

The TPA model presents the teaching act in a succinct, conceptually honest format. Since each skill or concept must have a teach component, a practice component, and an apply component, teachers can prepare and present a complete instructional sequence to ensure the mastery of the material. The feedback loop, or reteach, is an essential ingredient because it supplies a mechanism for teachers to monitor and provide corrective instruction for students who have not mastered the objective.

The TPA model helps teachers ensure student mastery and higher achievement scores because it integrates teaching, practice, and application activities along with the reteach loop into each lesson. The TPA format also encourages teachers to be flexible by developing and using additional teaching strategies. It can be used with a variety of teaching strategies to plan thorough, complete instructional sequences. Furthermore, the conceptual focus of TPA, when used in this way, provides teachers with the flexibility to select strategies that are most appropriate for the content as well as the needs of students. For example, teaching the long division steps may require a direct, step-by-step strategy while a problem-solving strategy may be more appropriate for teaching prime numbers. The combination of TPA and a variety of instructional strategies will help guarantee more appropriate and more effective instruction, and the result will be higher levels of student achievement.

Critical Thinking

An adequate knowledge base must be present in order to perceive and resolve problems. Cognitive learning theory suggests that new learning must be related to prior learning. If new data are presented to a student who has little or no prior knowledge of the topic, the data are perceived only as "noises." Critical thinking requires a knowledge base, and the TPA model can help develop it. Teachers must be careful, however, to avoid the fallacy that only after all basic skills have been acquired will a student be able to think critically. The development of the fourth R, critical thinking, should not occur after basics are mastered. Rather, it must take place simultaneously with basic skill development. Teachers who want their students to become critical thinkers and problem solvers integrate thought-provoking opportunities with basic skill instruction. They encourage students not only to learn facts, content, and skills, but also to apply new material to real-life situations in creative ways. In short, they help students go beyond convention, beyond the classroom, and beyond their present views.

A reading analogy will be helpful. It does little good to teach letter sounds if students cannot use the sounds to read. Further, teachers do not withhold books from beginning readers until they have completely mastered reading. Effective teachers provide books, often before students can read the words. They do this to encourage students to apply and extend their present skills.

The TPA model is an excellent vehicle for encouraging the integration of critical thinking skills into the daily instructional sequence. A good teach relates the current level of instruction to previous instruction; it also relates current instruction to events in students' personal lives. Thus, the basis for thinking is established because the teacher has made the lesson relevant to students' experience. Skills are not taught in isolation; they are related to the outside world and taught within the context of each student's existing knowledge base.

Practice provides students with an opportunity to strengthen skills initiated during the teach portion of the lesson. The strengthening of skills is necessary for achievement and also for the ability to think. Confused and ineffective thinking occurs when the problem solver is uncertain. Practice can reduce this uncertainty.

Practice is also essential to application, and it is at this level that critical thinking can really emerge. Once skills or concepts have been taught and practiced, students are ready to apply them at higher levels of thinking. During the apply portion of the lesson the teacher can move students to analysis, synthesis, and evaluation. As a matter of fact, students cannot really consider material at these higher levels until they have developed prerequisite understandings in the teach and practice phases.

Bloom (7) criticized U.S. schools because they seldom move students beyond learning basic information—they rarely require students to observe, reflect, or experiment. We believe that higher-level thinking can emerge in every teacher's classroom through the use of the apply portion of the lesson.

Critical thinking also relates to the concept of novelty—to unique and often humorous ways of viewing concepts. Novelty can emerge when people are allowed to use ideas playfully. The apply portion of the TPA model can incorporate opportunities for students to playfully and creatively consider material developed in the teach and practice phases.

The approach outlined in this text is premised on the notion that a thorough approach to instruction, coupled with alternative teaching strategies, will enhance teaching effectiveness. To this point we have considered critical thinking only in terms of Teach-Practice-Apply. The use of several teaching strategies allows the teacher the flexibility to help students learn in a variety of ways. Some topics are best learned through direct instruction; others may be more appropriately learned through discovery and experimentation.

Critical thinking can be nurtured by selecting the most appropriate teaching strategy. For those skills that are best learned through direct instruction, the use of discussion and problem-solving strategies would cause students needless frustration, thus inhibiting critical thinking. Interactive strategies such as concept attainment, problem solving, guided discussions, and simulations encourage students to relate past experiences and knowledge to the current task. They must relate, apply, integrate and evaluate. They must experiment, manipulate data, conclude, and consider novel applications. In short, they must think.

Student Attitudes

Perhaps the two school subjects least liked by elementary students, science and social studies, typify the negative effects of relying on a single instructional routine. In most science and social studies classes students are directed to read excerpts from a text and then answer questions at the end of the reading assignment. The problem-solving techniques of the physical and social sciences are missing. Instructional variety can stimulate students to learn in many different ways, even in science and social studies. Both student and teacher become more excited and motivated; and when students are excited, they are more attentive. Learning becomes challenging and the likelihood that they will look forward to school increases. A recent illustration of this concept: a teacher who stated that many of her students cried when school was canceled because of snow. Flexible, creative teaching can have a powerful effect on students.

PROFESSIONAL IMPROVEMENT AND INSTRUCTIONAL EFFECTIVENESS

One of the prevailing myths about teaching is that it does not require specific training; anyone who wants to teach, can. On the contrary, teaching is demanding, complex, and cognitive in nature; it is a profession that is rooted in research and shared practices. It requires decision-making skills, flexibility, and an ability to adapt and change. Professional and personal growth is a lifelong process, however. There are no quick fixes for developing a growth and renewal plan; there are only guidelines. For educators, professional self-improvement requires a deep desire to make changes in their teaching performance. Such a desire and commitment combined with the information presented in this book can lead to greater instructional efficacy.

Improvement in the schools occurs at both the teacher level and the school level. This book has addressed improvement at the teacher level. We believe that no matter how many directives the central office mandates, it is the individual teacher who makes change possible. Consequently, it is the teacher's responsibility to establish and implement a plan that fosters instructional improvement. Coaching, goal setting, and timing, which are briefly described in the following sections, can help teachers ''put things together'' instructionally.

Coaching

The magnitude of change may depend on the teacher's ability to accept feedback from peers, students, and supervisors. One way to initiate change—to apply and master new strategies—is to use a feedback system called coaching. Working in small teams, teachers ''coach'' one another as they try to work a skill into their teaching repertoire (33).

At first, until the rough edges are smoothed out, a new teaching strategy or suggestion may feel awkward. At this point the process of coaching becomes a useful feedback system for improving instruction, providing support, reconciling perceptions, and sharing mutual feelings and problems with colleagues. Working together in three- or four-member teams, teachers can demonstrate and practice a specific teaching strategy using the TPA format and receive the feedback of their peers. For example, team members may ask: ''Does the teacher present the material during the teach in an efficient and effective manner? During the apply, does the teacher provide for enrichment activities?'' Coaching also adds an element of companionship that encourages teachers to share their successes and frustrations and to work out problems that may have surfaced during demonstration sessions. Sharing concerns in a coaching setting can benefit all team members as they attempt to transfer newly learned pedagogical skills into their classrooms.

Setting Goals

Establishing personal and professional goals is another way to facilitate professional change. Just as they select instructional objectives to guide their lessons, effective teachers identify professional goals to guide their instructional performance. Self-knowledge is the first step in selecting reasonable and manageable goals. For example, what would you like to accomplish? Do you want to add one, two, or more new teaching strategies to your repertoire? In what curriculum areas? What time span do you think is feasible to initiate and successfully make a change? a grading period? a term? a year?

Timing

Once the professional goal or goals have been set, a time line should be developed outlining the order in which the goals will be implemented. Then a team of three or four coaches who have similar needs and goals should be formed. At regular meetings one team member at a time demonstrates a new strategy to be used in his/her classroom, as peer coaches assess and provide corrective feedback.

When the skills have been refined, teachers can transfer them to their classrooms where students become the second wave of assessors, providing comments and suggestions at teacher request. Teachers who feel uncomfortable can structure the process by asking students to respond in writing to written questions. Thus feedback from students and peers can assist in shaping the teacher's classroom delivery.

SUMMARY

Teachers are the key agents in the change process, as well as in the educative process. Our intent has been to provide new ideas and make several teaching strategies accessible to elementary teachers. By linking information about these strategies and TPA with teacher expertise in curriculum content and the learning process, professional and personal improvement is achievable.

Excellence in the classroom depends on the technical core discussed in Chapter 1 and the belief that this core of teaching skills does make a difference in the classroom. Research on effective teaching relates specific teacher behaviors to positive student outcomes and improved attitudes toward school. The teaching skills that make up the technical core are not new. What is new is the integration of these skills with the TPA model and the implementation of varied teaching strategies. Professional growth and change are managed gradually through the integration of these three rather diverse areas. For us, "Education . . . is not just something that happens in the head. It involves our muscles, our senses . . . our biochemistry. . . . Education springs from the interplay between the individual and a changing environment" (64, p. 13).

This book has used the TPA model as the framework to explain how effective teachers sequence instruction. It is hoped that the ideas shared, along with the many examples, checklists, and sections for applying knowledge, will stimulate teachers to evaluate their current instructional practices and motivate them to make changes where needed. Self-evaluation, the first step in setting up a long-term professional development plan, is a prerequisite of sustained teaching excellence. Excellence in the classroom does not come easily. It requires diligence and an individual commitment to a lifelong process of instructional improvement.

Bibliography

1. Akin, J. *Teacher Supply/Demand.* Career Planning and Placement Center of the Association for School, College and University Staffing (AS-CUS). Manhattan, Kans.: Kansas State University, 1985.
2. Arlin M. "Teacher Transition Can Disrupt Time Flow in Classrooms." *American Educational Research Journal* 16, no. 1 (Winter 1979): 42–56.
3. Ausubel, D. *Educational Psychology: A Cognitive View.* New York: Holt, Rinehart and Winston, 1968.
4. Barr, R., and Dreeben, R. "Instruction in Classrooms." In *Review of Research in Education,* vol. 5, edited by L. Shulman. Itasca, Ill: Peacock, 1977.
5. Bennett, N., and others. *The Quality of Pupil Learning Experiences.* Hillsdale, N.J.: Lawrence Erlbaum Associates, 1984.
6. Berliner, D. "The Half-Full Glass: A Review of Research on Teaching." *Using What We know About Teaching,* edited by P. L. Hosford. Alexandria, Va.: Association for Supervision and Curriculum Development, 1984.
7. Bloom, B. S. "The Search for Methods of Group Instruction as Effective as One-to-One Tutoring." *Educational Leadership* 41 no. 8 (1984): 4–17.
8. Brophy, J. E. *Advances in Teacher Effectiveness Research.* Occasional Paper No. 18. East Lansing, Mich.: College of Education, Michigan State University, 1979.
9. Bruner, J. *The Process of Education.* Cambridge, Mass.: Harvard University Press, 1960.
10. Caldwell, J. H.; Huitt, W. G.; and Graeber, A. O. "Time Spent in Learning: Implications from Research." *Elementary School Journal* 82, no. 5 (1982): 471–79.
11. Coats, W., and Smidchens, U. "Audience Recall as a Function of Speaker Dynamism." *Journal of Educational Psychology* 57 (1986): 189–91.
12. Cooper, J. D., and others. *The What and How of Reading Instruction.* Columbus, Ohio: Charles E. Merrill Publishing Co., 1979.
13. Costa, A. L. "Recent Research on the Analysis of Instruction." *Practical Applications of Research* 2, no. 2 (December 1979). Bloomington, Ind.: Phi Delta Kappa.
14. Dawe, H. A. "Teaching: A Performing Art." *Phi Delta Kappan* 65 (April 1984): 548–52.
15. Denham, D., and Lieberman, A. *Time to Learn.* Sacramento, Calif.: Commission for Teacher Preparation and Licensing, 1980.
16. Dewey, J. *Democracy and Education: An Introduction to the Philosophy of Education.* New York: Free Press, 1966.
17. Durkin, D. "What Classroom Observation Reveals About Reading Comprehension Instruction." *Reading Research Quarterly* 14 (1978–1979): 481–533.
18. _____. "Reading Comprehension Instruction in Five Basal Reading Series." *Reading Research Quarterly* 4 (1981): 515–44.
19. Edney, J. J. "The Nuts Game: A Concise Common Dilemma An

alog." *Environmental Psychology and Nonverbal Behavior* 3, no. 4 (1979): 252-54.

20. Eisner, E. "The Art and Craft of Teaching." *Educational Leadership* 40, no. 4 (January 1983): 4-14.

21. Elkind, D. "Child Development and the Social Science Curriculum of the Elementary School." *Social Education* 45, no. 6 (October 1981): 435-37.

22. Gage, N. *The Scientific Basis for the Art of Teaching.* New York: Teachers College Press, 1977.

23. Gage, N. L., and Berliner, D. *Educational Psychology.* 3d ed. Boston: Houghton Mifflin Co., 1984.

24. Gall, M. D.; Dunning, B.; and Weathersby, R. *Higher Cognitive Questioning Teacher's Handbook.* Beverly Hills, Calif.: Macmillan Educational Services (for Far West Regional Laboratory), 1971.

25. Good, T. L., and Grouws, D. A. "The Missouri Mathematics Effectiveness Project." *Journal of Educational Psychology* 71 (1979): 355-62.

26. Goodlad, J. *A Place Called School.* New York: McGraw-Hill, 1983.

27. Greenblatt, Ruth B; Cooper, Bruce S.; and Muth, Rodney. "Managing for Effective Teaching." *Educational Leadership* (February 1984): 55.

28. Heiman, Marcia, and Slomianko, Joshua. *Critical Thinking Skills.* Washington, D.C.: National Education Association, 1986.

29. Hoover, K. H., and Hollingsworth, P. M. *A Handbook for Elementary School Teachers.* Abridged 2d ed. Boston: Allyn and Bacon, 1978.

30. Hosford, P. "The Silent Curriculum: Its Impact on Teaching the Basics." *Educational Leadership* (December 1978): 213.

31. Imig, D. G. "Renewal and Purpose." *AACTE Briefs* 5, no. 2 (March 1984).

32. Joyce, B. "Models of Teaching: Expanding the Teacher's Repertoire." National Curriculum Studies Institutes Workshop, Dallas, Texas, January 1983.

33. Joyce, B., and Showers, B. "The Coaching of Teaching." *Educational Leadership* 40, no. 1 (1982): 4-10.

34. Joyce, B., and Weil, M. *Models of Teaching.* Englewood Cliffs, N.J.: Prentice-Hall, 1980.

35. Kamii, C. "Teachers' Autonomy and Scientific Training." *Young Children* 36 (May 1981): 5-14.

36. Kennedy, J. J., and others. "Additional Investigations into the Nature of Teacher Clarity." *Journal of Educational Research* 72 (September–October 1978): 3-10.

37. Kounin, J. *Discipline and Group Management in Classrooms.* New York: Holt, Rinehart and Winston, 1970.

37a. Kunz, John. *Mathematics Made Meaningful with Cuisenaire Rods.* Cuisenaire Corporation of America, 12 13th St., P.O. Box D, New Rochelle, NY 10805.

38. Lapp, D., and others. *Teaching and Learning: Philosophical, Psychological, Curricular Applications.* New York: Macmillan, 1975.

39. Manatt, R. P. *Evaluating Teacher Performance.* Videotape. Washington, D.C.: Association for Supervision and Curriculum Development, 1981.

40. _____. "Manatt's Exercise in Selecting Teacher Performance Evaluation Criteria Based on Effective Teaching Research." National

Symposium for Professionals in Evaluation and Research, Albuquerque, N.M., November 1981.

41. Martin, R. J., and Van Cleaf, D. W. "Language Arts Students Improve Writing Skills." *Catalyst for Change* 12, no. 2 (1983): 17-18.
42. Maxim, G. M. *Methods of Teaching Social Studies to Elementary School Children* (p. 53). Columbus, Ohio: Charles E. Merrill, 1977.
43. Medley, D. *Teacher Competence and Teacher Effectiveness: A Review of Process-Product Research.* Washington, D.C.: American Association of Colleges for Teacher Education, 1977.
44. _____. *Teacher Competency Testing the Teacher Educators.* Charlottesville, Va.: Educational Research, School of Education, University of Virginia, 1982.
45. Michaelis, J. U.; Grossman, R. H.; and Scott, L. F. *New Designs for Elementary Curriculum and Instruction.* New York: McGraw-Hill, 1975.
46. McDonald, F. J. "Research on Teaching: A Report on Phase II of the Beginning Teacher Evaluation Study." In *The Appraisal of Teaching: Concepts and Processes,* edited by Gary D. Borich and Kathleen S. Fenton. Reading, Mass.: Addison-Wesley, 1977.
47. McFaul, S. A. "An Examination of Direct Instruction." *Educational Leadership* (April 1983).
48. National Commission on Excellence in Education. *A Nation at Risk: The Imperative for Educational Reform.* Washington, D.C.: U.S. Department of Education, 1983.
49. Peterson, P. L., and Walberg, H. L., eds. *Research on Teaching: Concepts, Findings and Implications.* Berkeley, Calif.: McCutchan, 1979.
50. Reinhartz, J. "To Know Why: Systematic Science Curriculum Through Learning Centers." *Science Education* 62, no. 2 (1978): 153-64.
51. Reinhartz, Judy, ed. *Perspectives on Effective Teaching and the Cooperative Classroom.* Washington, D.C.: National Education Association, 1984.
52. Reinhartz, J., and Beach, D. M. *Improving Middle School Instruction: A Research-Based Self-Assessment System.* Washington, D.C.: National Education Association, 1983.
53. Reynolds, J. "In Search of Mr. (Ms.) Goodteacher." *Action in Teacher Education* 11, no. 1 (Winter 1979-1980): 35-38.
54. Rosenshine, B. "Content, Time, and Direct Instruction." In *Research on Teaching: Concepts, Findings and Implications,* edited by P. Peterson and H. L. Walberg. Berkeley, Calif.: McCutchan, 1979.
55. _____. "Teaching Functions in Instructional Programs." *Elementary School Journal* 83 (1983): 335-52.
56. _____, and Furst, N. "Research in Teacher Performance Criteria." In *Research in Teacher Education,* edited by B. O. Smith. Englewood Cliffs, N.J.: Prentice-Hall, 1971.
57. Rouk, U. "Separate Studies Show Similar Results of Teacher Effectiveness." *Education R & D Report* 2, no. 2 (Spring 1979): 6-10.
58. Rowe, M. B. "Wait Time and Rewards as Instructional Variables, Their Influence on Language, Logic and Fate Control: Part One—Wait Time." *Journal of Research in Science Teaching* 11 (1974): 81-94.
59. Rubin, L. "Artistry in Teaching." *Educational Leadership* 40, no. 4 (January 1983): 44-51.
60. Ryans, D. G. *Characteristics of Teachers.* Washington, D.C.: American Council on Education, 1960.

60a. Sanders, Norris M. *Classroom Questions: What Kinds?* New York: Harper and Row, 1966.

61. Soar, R., and Soar, R. "Classroom Behavior, Pupil Characteristics, and Pupil Growth for the School Year and for the Summer." *JSAS Catalog of Selected Documents in Psychology*, vol. 5, 1975, 200-MS. University of Florida.

62. Solomon, D.; Bezdek, W.; and Rosenberg, L. *Teaching Styles and Learning.* Chicago, Ill.: Center for the Study of Liberal Education for Adults, 1963.

63. Stallings, J. "Teaching Basic Reading Skills in the Secondary Schools." Paper presented at Annual Meeting of American Educational Research Association, 1978.

64. Toffler, A. "The Psychology of the Future." *Learning for Tomorrow: The Role of the Future in Education,* edited by A. Toffler. New York: Vintage Books, 1974.

65. Van Cleaf, D. "Guiding Student Inquiry." *Social Studies* (May–June 1984).

66. Van Cleaf, D. W., and Pippin, G. D. "Thinking About the Heart." *Health Education,* in press.

67. Van Cleaf, D., and Reinhartz, J. "Teach, Practice, and Apply: A Step Beyond Direct Instruction." Unpublished manuscript, 1985.

68. Walberg, H. J.; Schiller, D.; and Haertel, G. D. "The Quiet Revolution in Educational Research." *Phi Delta Kappan* 61 (November 1979): 179–83.

69. Wilen, W. W. *Questioning Skills, for Teachers.* 2d ed. Washington, D.C.: National Education Association, 1986.

70. Zevin, J. "Mystery Island: A Lesson in Inquiry." *Today's Education* 58 (1969): 42–43.